Royal Victoria Country Park, Netley.

Shire County Guide 24

HAMPSHIRE

Adrian Rance

Shire Publications Ltd

CONTENTS

Printed in Great Britain by C. I. Thomas & Sons (Haverfordwest) Ltd, Press Buildings, Merlins Bridge, Haverfordwest, Dyfed SA61 1XF.

British Library Cataloguing in Publication Data available.

Cover: *The farmhouse of Manor Farm, Upper Hamble Country Park, now the Hampshire Farm Museum.*

ACKNOWLEDGEMENTS
Photographs are acknowledged as follows: Broadlands (Romsey) Limited, page 34; Cadbury Lamb, pages 2, 3, 6, 11, 17, 21, 22, 24, 25, 28, 29, 30, 31, 33, 36, 39, 43, 45, 46, 49, 50, 51, 53, 54, 57, 58, 63; Ocean Village, page 2; Anne Ruffell, page 59; Southampton City Council, pages 23, 41, 55. All the rest are by the author.

Ocean Village, in the Old Docks, Southampton.

Beaulieu Abbey across the lake.

1
An introduction to Hampshire

Although Winchester is the capital city of Hampshire, the county takes its name from Hamtun, the seventh-century predecessor of Southampton. The abbreviation, Hants, comes from a version of the name *Hamtunscire,* written down by a Norman scribe.

Hampshire covers 1382 square miles (3580 sq km). It is a county of contrasts rather than extremes. From the rolling countryside in the centre of the county with historic Winchester at its heart, to the spacious heathlands of the New Forest, the shores of the Solent or the great towns of Southampton and Portsmouth, the visitor finds a variety and quality which is probably unequalled in the United Kingdom.

Many visitors pass through Hampshire without pausing to explore its riches. Whether on the road to the docks of Portsmouth and Southampton, thence to foreign climes, or heading for the tourist destinations of the West Country, many visitors enter the county along the M3, which reaches in an unbroken run from London to Winchester, and continue from there by dual carriageway to Southampton or the New Forest. Travelling the road may be a great benefit to the motorist but a special effort must be made to explore the historic cities, the elegant Georgian market towns, the picturesque villages, the yacht havens of the Solent and the open spaces of

countryside which may otherwise be ignored.

A COUNTY OF CONTRASTS

It is easier to appreciate the contrast between the centre and the north of the county when approaching from the south, perhaps up the Candover valley from the picturesque market town of Alresford. From the quaintly named Farleigh Wallop you can view the whole of the north Hampshire plain with its sprawling heathlands, where the clay of the Reading beds and the sands of the Bagshot beds separate the chalk countryside of central Hampshire from the borders of Berkshire. Here there are Farnborough and Aldershot, both famous for their association with the defence of the realm. Large country houses such as The Vyne, run by the National Trust, and Stratfield Saye, given by a grateful nation to the first Duke of Wellington, are just some of the rich crop that might be missed on a journey south.

The central part of Hampshire is dominated by the massive block of chalkland which is, in effect, an eastward extension of Salisbury Plain. On the north side of this chalk triangle the land rises to a height of 800 feet (250 metres) where the chalk of the Hampshire Downs ascends sharply before plunging down below the younger rocks of the North Hamp-

3

shire Plain. Again, south of Winchester the chalk disappears below the Tertiary strata although it does reappear in the form of the Portsdown Hill Ridge just north of Portsmouth. A number of rivers, notably the Test and the Itchen, flow south from the heart of the chalklands through some of the most luxuriant countryside in the county. Waymarked trails have been created to help the walker explore the countryside of central Hampshire.

The New Forest is unique. Here the soft sandy and clayey post-chalk Tertiary rocks have produced a countryside in which dense woodland alternates with wild heathlands. The history of the New Forest, together with its special landscape and natural history, make it the destination of millions of tourists each year.

The statue of King Alfred by Hamo Thornycroft, erected in the Broadway, Winchester, in 1901.

The coastal plain of Hampshire provides its own contrasts. The combination of sea erosion and the rise in sea level in the neolithic period has created Southampton Water, the Solent, the Hamble and Beaulieu estuaries, and Portsmouth and Langstone harbours. The sheltered estuaries and creeks, salt marshes and tidal mud flats, each with its own rich and varied wildlife, contrast with the great seaports of Portsmouth and Southampton.

DEFENCE OF THE REALM

Hampshire is a maritime county and, from the days of Henry V to D-Day in 1944, the people of Hampshire have seen armies depart from its shores. The county has a unique history in the defence of the realm, a history that can be enjoyed in the military museums of the garrison towns, the naval museums of Gosport and Portsmouth, aircraft museums, and fortifications which include the Roman fort at Portchester, the medieval defences of Southampton, the castles built by Henry VIII, and the massive Victorian forts designed to protect Portsmouth and the Solent. With oak from New Forest trees, Hampshire craftsmen built the wooden walls of Nelson's navy. But now the tidal rivers are crowded with thousands of yachts belonging to those who seek peace or enjoyment on the sheltered waters of the Solent.

There is a remarkable diversity of urban development in the towns of Hampshire. In the north there are the urban sprawls of the military towns and the postwar London overspills of Andover and Basingstoke. In the heart of the county there is the historic city of Winchester, dominated by its cathedral. Small, elegant market towns, with broad main streets and squares flanked by the brick frontages of countless Georgian houses, are found all over Hampshire from the seaside town of Lymington in the south to Hartley Wintney in the north. Then there are the great industrial seaports of Portsmouth and Southampton: the one was a garrison town built around a naval base; the other is famous for its associations with the great liners. Both Portsmouth and Southampton are large modern towns but each has a fascinating choice of attractions for the visitor. Portsmouth is now world-famous for its heritage associated with the defence of the realm. Southampton has a unique collection of medieval monuments, including the extensive town walls and, with its shopping centre, its parks and its gardens, is an ideal base for visiting Hampshire. Both towns are now well established on the tourist trail.

Many factors have fashioned the Hampshire of today and perhaps there is no other county in which the huge variety of natural and historic heritage is so carefully managed and presented for the benefit of visitors.

4

The Rufus Stone in the New Forest.

2
The countryside and coast

THE NEW FOREST

The New Forest can be explored in the car, on foot, on bicycles or even on horseback. The natural landscape of the Forest itself has three elements: the heathlands of the high, windswept plateaux, the wooded slopes and the lower-lying marshy land. Within the landscape there are towns and villages, chief of which is Lyndhurst, the home of the Verderers' Court, which has been part of the judicial and administrative hierarchy since Norman times and still controls many aspects of forest life and its economy. Lymington is the port of the New Forest and is now a favourite base for yachtsmen. In 1724 Daniel Defoe described the trade of the area: 'smuggling and roguing [are] the reigning commerce of this part of the English coast.'

The recreational use of the New Forest is controlled by a management plan which aims to permit the maximum enjoyment by visitors without allowing the Forest's character to change. After all, the Forest is unique in the world for its historical associations, its natural history and the antiquity of its living traditions. Over 130 car parks and camp sites are carefully sited and are well signposted from all the roads. Motor access is limited to these areas to

minimise damage by the many thousands of vehicles that visit the Forest each year. Visitors are encouraged to walk within the Forest and waymarked walks are provided to guide the inexperienced.

The unenclosed Forest woodlands are the finest relics of undisturbed deciduous forest in western Europe. The so-called 'Inclosures' are areas of managed woodland which have been producing timber for many centuries. These include the plantations of oak created in the early nineteenth century to meet the anticipated demands of the Royal Navy (which turned to iron-built ships long before the trees had matured).

The natural history of the New Forest can be enjoyed and studied in many places but perhaps the most accessible is the **Deer Sanctuary** at Boldrewood. The visitor can not only explore the extensive nineteenth-century plantation and arboretum, but special platforms have been constructed to permit viewing of the herds of deer that congregate there.

A few miles to the west of Lyndhurst, at Holiday's Hill, there is the **New Forest Reptilery** run by the Forestry Commission (telephone: 042128 3141). Specially constructed habitats contain examples of the adder, the

5

Mottisfont Abbey.

grass snake and slow-worm and other native New Forest reptiles. They are not easy to see amid the moss and leaves but for most visitors this is their only chance to see these little creatures of the forest.

The best way to explore the New Forest is by using a guide produced by the Forestry Commission and published by the HMSO. It is called *Explore the New Forest* and is divided into manageable walks, each one accompanied by a section of the 1:25,000 Ordnance Survey map. The New Forest Tourist Information Service is at the New Forest Museum and Visitor Centre (see chapter 8), Lyndhurst Car Park (telephone: 042128 2888).

THE TEST WAY

The Test Way is a waymarked walk that stretches from Totton on Southampton Water to Inkpen Beacon in the north. The first stretch is along the broad valley of the Test reaching from Redbridge, where the tidal river begins, through **Nursling** and past the estates of Broadlands (see chapter 6), up to the market town of Romsey. Just beyond Nursling (in the churchyard is the tomb of the great archaeologist. Ò. G. S. Crawford), the walk cuts across the valley to proceed along its western edge on its way to Romsey. Many of the villages in the Test valley end their name with the element 'bridge', indicating their ancient importance as a crossing over the river. Awbridge and Kimbridge, for instance, are on the route before Mottisfont, with its priory, is reached (see chapter 6). Then the path follows the line of the disused Andover to Romsey railway for about 10 miles (16 km); it skirts the little town of Stockbridge, but the visitor

would be well advised to detour and explore the interesting and elegant High Street (see chapter 11). Before reaching Stockbridge, the walker will go close by Marsh Court, a great white house designed by Sir Edwin Lutyens and now a school. The gardens were designed by Gertrude Jekyll and can be visited by appointment (see chapter 6).

The Test Way continues north along the line of the disused railway to the village of **Leckford**, which was bought by the John Lewis Partnership in 1928 and now provides rest and recreation for the many partners in that enlightened firm. Some of the finest views in Hampshire are to be enjoyed along this stretch of the Test Way. The route soon brings the walker to the little village of **Wherwell**, the site of Wherwell Priory, founded in AD 986 by Queen Elfrida.

Just before the village of Longparish, the path rises up from the river valley, skirting Harwood Forest until it reaches the Bourne Valley. From here there is a splendid view of the little village of St Mary Bourne in whose church there is one of the eight known fonts made in the twelfth century of marble from Tournai.

As the Test Way climbs into the Hampshire highlands, the walker looking back will see an idyllic vision of an English country village nestling in the folds of the gentle hills. Up through the historic village of Hurstbourne Tarrant and **Ibthorpe**, well known to Jane Austen as the home of her friend Martha Lloyd, the path reaches up to the chalk escarpment topped by Inkpen Hill and Combe Gibbet with breathtaking views over the Kennet valley some 300 feet (90 metres) below: a

6

dramatic conclusion to a walk of almost 50 miles (80 km).

THE CLARENDON WAY

This ancient route, which connects the cathedral cities of Winchester and Salisbury, is a waymarked walk through some of the finest countryside of Wiltshire and Hampshire.

A good starting point for the Hampshire section is the village of **Broughton**, near the church of St Mary. Here there is a fascinating dovecote which is worth a visit. The path runs along the valley, of the Wallop Brook before reaching Bossington where this little tributary joins the river Test. Rising out of the Test valley, the route crosses the Test Way and reaches the village of Kings Somborne, from where it climbs up to the high lands of Beacon Hill and Farley Mount. The Clarendon Way continues throughout the length of the Farley Mount Country Park (see below), skirting past Crab Wood, which contains the Sparsholt Roman Villa, the subject of archaeological investigation. The Way then turns towards Stanmore and passes through Oliver's Battery into the cathedral city of Winchester.

THE SOLENT WAY

The Solent Way is a long-distance walk along 60 miles (95 km) of Hampshire's coast, beginning at **Milford-on-Sea** in the west and finishing at Emsworth on the Sussex border.

Milford was once an inland village and the erosion of the coastline which gave it a seafront continues to this day. Here there are spectacular views across the Solent to the Isle of Wight. Just to the east there is the massive bank of pebbles, 1½ miles (2.5 km) long, known as Hurst Spit, with Hurst Castle at its furthest limit (see chapter 5). From Hurst the walker can take a ferry which wends its way through the waterways, between mudflats, to the little village of **Keyhaven**, now much beloved by yachtsmen. From Keyhaven the walk follows the line of a sea wall for the 5 miles (8 km) to the town of Lymington (see chapter 11). The Keyhaven, Pennington and Lymington Marshes are a haven of wildlife with large numbers of native and migratory birds.

The Way crosses the Lymington River by the old eighteenth-century causeway and climbs past Walhampton House, now a school and once famous for its gardens designed in the picturesque tradition. From here the Solent Way remains inland although there are occasional glimpses of the Solent. On the way to Buckler's Hard (see chapter 11) the walk passes Sowley Pond, originally a fish pond of Beaulieu Abbey, but in the seventeenth and eighteenth centuries a source of power for an important ironworks. Beaulieu, with its abbey,

motor museum, village and tide mill can take up the best part of a day (see chapters 4, 6, 8 and 11), but the intrepid walker will continue the Solent Way across the wild and desolate expanse of Beaulieu Heath to the village of **Hythe** on the New Forest shore of Southampton Water. The route misses the coastal areas of Exbury (see chapter 6), Lepe, Calshot Spit and its sixteenth-century castle (see chapter 5) and Fawley. Each of these is worth visiting on foot, bicycle or by car.

The first steam ferry linking Southampton to Hythe started operating in the 1820s and a ferry still runs a regular service between Hythe Pier and Southampton's Town Quay. The Solent Way walker can spend a whole day exploring the historic town of Southampton with its waterfront, museums, historic monuments and town walls (see chapters 3, 4, 5, 6, 8 and 11). However, crossing the soaring and elegant bridge over the river Itchen, the trail then proceeds down the eastern side of Southampton Water into Woolston. Here the long history of shipbuilding continues today with the sprawling works of Vosper Thornycroft, who have been building warships here for over eighty years.

The walk from Woolston to Hamble passes down Weston Shore, with its fine beaches, to Netley, famous for its medieval abbey (see chapter 4) and the Royal Victoria Country Park, site of the gigantic Netley Military Hospital built after the Crimean War. One is often rewarded with the sight of great cargo ships or liners such as the *Queen Elizabeth II* passing up or down Southampton Water as one walks this stretch of the Solent Way.

The river Hamble is now well known as a yachting centre. More yachts are found on this river than on any other comparable inlet; there are forests of masts in the numerous marinas. At Hamble the walker can summon the small ferry which crosses the river to Warsash on the opposite shore. From Warsash the walk follows almost 6 miles (10 km) of coast with few indications of human presence. The Hook-with-Warsash Nature Reserve and Titchfield Haven are both sanctuaries for all sorts of wildlife. The coastal walk here is secluded and peaceful, all the more surprising considering the proximity of two of England's busiest ports.

Hill Head, with its fine views across to the Isle of Wight, is at the entrance to Titchfield Haven and the valley of the river Meon; from here a continuous shingle beach stretches down to Gosport. First **Lee-on-the-Solent** is reached, the home of the Royal Naval Air Service station, HMS *Daedalus*.

As the Solent Way comes to Gosport (see chapter 11) one is reminded of the great ring of artillery fortifications that surround both Gosport and Portsmouth (see chapter 5), with Fort

7

Gilliker and the star-shaped Fort Monkton. Fort Brockhurst is somewhat off the course of the Way but well worth a detour (see chapter 5).

A ferry travels across the narrow stretch of water between Gosport and Portsmouth which forms the entrance to Portsmouth Harbour. The ferry journey gives an opportunity to appreciate the extent of the Naval Dockyard where modern warships lie alongside magnificent eighteenth-century dockyard buildings (see chapter 8). The many and varied attractions of Old Portsmouth are described elsewhere (see chapters 4 and 11).

Southsea, with its long esplanade and Clarence Pier, was a fashionable suburb to Old Portsmouth and became popular as a seaside holiday resort earlier in the twentieth century. It is the nearest approach to a traditional holiday sea front on the Solent Way and includes the great attractions of Southsea Castle and the D-Day Museum. The Solent Way continues past Fort Cumberland, the best example of eighteenth-century defensive architecture in the United Kingdom (see chapter 5), and soon comes to Eastney on the eastern tip of Portsea Island. Here there is the Eastney Pumping Station with its impressive beam engines (see chapter 7).

Langstone Harbour on the east of Portsea Island mirrors Portsmouth Harbour on the west. However, whereas there are naval ships in one, the other is an outstanding nature reserve. Nearly 5000 acres (2020 ha) of tidal water and mudlands and a shoreline of 16 miles (26 km) make this one of the most impressive sections of the Solent Way. At the top of the harbour the route passes round the **Farlington Marshes**, a nature reserve run by the County Council and the Hampshire and Isle of Wight Naturalists Trust, and where there is a wide variety of wildfowl. The little quay at Langstone, dominated by a former windmill, is picturesque and lonely. The walk is almost over here for it just has to skirt past Warblington before it reaches the historic port of **Emsworth** where Hampshire gives way to the jurisdiction of Sussex.

THE WAYFARERS' WALK

Emsworth is the start of a 70 mile (110 km) signposted walk across the heart of the county to Inkpen Beacon where the highlands of Hampshire look out over Berkshire and which is also the finishing point of the Test Way. The Walk has been created linking public footpaths, bridleways, green lanes, ancient trackways and the occasional road.

The first section crosses the fields to Warblington church, with its gruesome gravewatchers' huts (see chapter 4) and from here the path follows the north shore of Langstone Harbour. At Bedhampton the walker has to

use the road to climb to the top of Portsdown Hill before cutting across country, through fields and woods to Denmead, home of the famous pottery (see chapter 9). Hambledon, the home of the national game of cricket, is the next village (see chapter 11).

From Hambledon the walk passes across farmland before descending into the picturesque Meon valley at Soberton. The walk follows the river to **Droxford**, a delightful village with its cluster of brick Georgian houses. Here there are the remains of the Alton to Fareham railway line which was opened in 1903. On the nights before the liberation of Europe in 1944, Churchill and his chiefs of staff stayed in their special train at Droxford Station.

The Walk climbs from the valley to the South Hampshire Ridgeway high on the chalk, passing through woodland of quality and a place with the intriguing name of Betty Mundy's Bottom. The Ridgeway itself is part of a prehistoric route which crosses southern England from Kent to Salisbury. From the chalk ridge, with its panoramic views across to Cheriton and New Alresford, the route crosses to Kilmeston and thence to Hinton Ampner with its manor and gardens owned by the National Trust (see chapter 6).

The village of **Cheriton**, often the holder of 'best kept village' awards, with the river Itchen running through the village green, is notable for its associations with the battle of Cheriton, fought on 29th March 1644. The neighbouring village of **Tichborne** is well remembered for the celebrated case of the 'Tichborne claimant', who claimed to be the Victorian heir to the estate who mysteriously vanished en route to Australia.

The walk passes through Alresford (see chapter 11) and, after refreshment at the excellent inns or tea houses, the walker can proceed to Itchen Stoke Down along the ancient Drove Lane, along which thousands of sheep were driven to Alresford market in bygone years. It passes the deserted medieval village of Abbotstone where humps and bumps in a field are all that is left of the houses and streets of a once flourishing community. From here the old drove roads are followed across the chalk downs: one is called the Lunway, an ancient trackway across the chalklands of central England.

Along the Candover valley to the ridge above Brown Candover, Preston Candover and Chilton Candover, the trail passes along a good track before descending again to the village of Dummer. From here the walk rises again to the crest of the North Hampshire Ridgeway, a prehistoric track across the ridge of the North Hampshire chalk downs. The turf is ideal for horses and the walk takes one past the famous gallops of White Hill. From here it

Southampton Water at Calshot.

crosses the now famous Watership Down before passing the iron age hillfort on Ladle Hill and descending to Seven Barrows near the A34 south of Beacon Hill (see chapter 3).

The last part of the magnificent walk is again a slow climb to the high ground, passing above Highclere, with its parks laid out by 'Capability' Brown, until the walker comes at last to Combe Gibbet and Inkpen Beacon, the great heights from which Hampshire looks down into the lowlands of Berkshire.

COUNTRY PARKS
Farley Mount Country Park, Sarum Road, Winchester. Telephone: 0962 64221. Hampshire County Council.

Part of the old route between Winchester and Salisbury, the Clarendon Way, runs through this part of Hampshire's chalk downlands which is now managed as a country park. Here there are miles of country walks through woodland and downland, much of it protected as a site of special scientific interest. One strange feature of the park is a pyramid-shaped monument set on the top of a prominent hill. It was raised as a tombstone to a horse that in 1733 saved his master from a dreadful accident by jumping a 25 foot (8 metre) chalk pit. The views from Farley Mount are glorious on a fine day.

There are facilities at Farley Mount for group barbecues which can be booked in advance.

Itchen Navigation
The difference between a navigation and a canal is that the former employs the natural course of a river for much of its length. The Itchen Navigation was established in the latter part of the seventeenth century to connect Winchester and the port of Southampton for the transport of bulk cargoes such as coal. The last barge travelled on the route in the 1860s.

Although the towpath is not maintained as a walk it is possible to travel the entire length from Northam Bridge in Southampton to Winchester. The industrial archaeology of the navigation is of considerable interest (see chapter 7), but for those who enjoy the countryside it is an ideal way to experience the valley of the river Itchen with its extensive water meadows. The walk takes only half a day.

Lepe Country Park, Lepe, Exbury. Telephone: office 0962 846034, Ranger 0703 899108. Hampshire County Council.

This is an ideal place from which to enjoy and admire the New Forest coast, looking out at the yachts and the shipping of the Solent and the views of the Isle of Wight. Lepe has one of the few sandy beaches on the Hampshire coast and there are excellent refreshment facilities.

The Country Park continues along the popular beach of Calshot Spit. The shipping lane is only a few hundred yards offshore and the

9

massive tankers moving up to Fawley oil refinery make an impressive sight. Calshot is not only famous for its sixteenth-century castle (see chapter 5) but also for its history as a flying boat base between 1913 and the 1950s. Now the flying boat hangers are owned by the County Council which runs an activities centre there with facilities for indoor cycling, skiing, sailing and a host of other sports.

Queen Elizabeth Country Park, Gravel Hill, Horndean. On either side of the A3 south of Petersfield. Telephone: 0705 595040. Hampshire County Council.

The Queen Elizabeth Country Park is on the east side of the county and covers more than 1000 acres (400 ha).

The Park Centre, which houses exhibitions and an audio-visual theatre, is at the entrance to the forest on the east side of the A3 road. There are a number of waymarked trails across the hills which include a modern beech forest with a woodland drive to a picnic area at the top. The wildlife is plentiful; the observant, and not too noisy, walker will be able to see deer as they cross the firebreaks in the woodland.

From the woodland an underpass takes the visitor to the open downland of Butser Hill, which forms the western end, and the highest part of, the South Downs. The open downland with its rich variety of wild flowers, the deep coombes and massive slopes are unique in the county. The Ancient Farm Project, which has been re-creating rural life of the iron age, while carrying out exhaustive experiments in prehistoric farming techniques and animal husbandry, can be visited on Little Butser (see chapter 3). For those of a more energetic disposition the modern sports of grass skiing and hang-gliding regularly take place on the steep slopes.

Royal Victoria Country Park, Netley Abbey, Southampton SO3 5GA. Telephone: 0703 455157. Hampshire County Council.

The military hospital on the shore of Southampton Water at Netley was over a quarter of a mile (400 metres) long. It was built after the Crimean War and served in the Boer Wars and the First and Second World Wars. The only part of the main building to be spared demolition is the chapel whose tower dominates many early photographs of Southampton Water. The chapel now houses an exhibition which explains the long, fascinating and often tragic history of the hospital. A stairway and lift allow visitors to ascend to the top of the tower from which there are breathtaking views across the water to the New Forest.

The Country Park has been created to enable visitors to enjoy the views and beaches that were previously the preserve of staff and patients at Netley. There are extensive walks along the beach and in the woodlands that once surrounded the hospital.

Upper Hamble Country Park, Pylands Road, Bursledon SO3 8BH. Telephone: 0703 455157. Hampshire County Council.

The Upper Hamble Country Park has been created to provide access to the delightful countryside along the upper reaches of the river. There are extensive walks along the grassy river banks and muddy creeks which in the Second World War housed secret camps used by Marines training for the liberation of Europe. There are other walks through the woodlands between Bursledon (see chapter 11) and the village of Botley to the north. The County Council is currently restoring a walk along the east bank which will continue down to Warsash, passing the village of Bursledon with its shipyards which have a history stretching back to the days when the ships of Nelson's navy were built on the banks of the river.

The Hampshire Farm Museum at Manor Farm, Botley, lies within the Country Park and should be included in a visit (see chapter 8).

Yateley Common Country Park, Yateley. On the A30 north-east of Hartley Wintney. Telephone: 0252 874346. Hampshire County Council.

Yateley Common is Hampshire's largest common. The 500 acres (200 ha) of heathland are but a fragment of a vast heather moor which once covered the area. The main road between London and the West Country (now superseded by the M3) was the haunt of highwaymen and smugglers in former times when coaches travelled the lonely route. During the Second World War some of the common was taken over as an airfield, later famous as Blackbushe Airport.

The survival of so much open ground in a part of Britain which has been very extensively developed is a great pleasure. A nature trail around Wyndham's Pool takes the walker through heather, gorse thicket, woodlands and low-lying ponds and bogs.

The Ancient Farm Project at Butser Hill, Queen Elizabeth Country Park.

3
The archaeology of Hampshire

STONE AGE

Unlike the neighbouring county of Wiltshire, there are in Hampshire few sites to visit from the early prehistoric periods. However, the county's museum collections abound with palaeolithic flint axes from the gravel terraces of the rivers Test and Itchen. Field work in recent years has filled out the picture for the mesolithic period when hunter-gatherers roamed the chalk downlands and were able to wander dry-shod across to the Isle of Wight.

The prominent monuments from the neolithic period are the earthen long barrows which vary in length in Hampshire from about 100 feet (30 metres) to about 300 feet (95 metres). These great communal works of neolithic society were clearly used for burial, although they may have had other ritual functions. Forty earthen long barrows have been identified in Hampshire, all of which are located on the chalk, in prominent positions, visible from long distances. There are two groups: one in the west of the county and a second group running across the Test valley towards the Itchen valley.

Danebury Long Barrows, Nether Wallop (OS 185; SU 320383).

An important concentration of three long barrows lies in the parish of Nether Wallop.

The approach for two is from beside the trees at Down Farm. These are under rough grass. A third ploughed barrow is in the field east of the farm.

Duck's Nest Long Barrow, Rockbourne (OS 184; SU 104204). In a prominent group of yew trees east of the road north of Rockbourne to Coombe Bissett.

This barrow is almost 130 feet (40 metres) long and is remarkable for the fact that it survives to a height of up to 15 feet (4.5 metres) above the side ditches, which are clearly defined.

Giant's Grave Long Barrow, Breamore (OS 184; SU 139200). North-east of the Castle Ditches hillfort, Whitsbury.

The barrow measures some 180 feet (54 metres) by 80 feet (24 metres) and stands to a height of about 10 feet (3 metres) although much of the west end has been damaged.

Grans Barrow Long Barrow, Rockbourne (OS 184; SU 090198). Just over half a mile (just under a kilometre) to the west of the Rockbourne to Coombe Bissett road.

The barrow is about 180 feet (55 metres) long and survives to a height of 8 feet (2.5

metres). Under grass, it is one of the best preserved barrows in the county.

Knap Barrow Long Barrow, Martin (OS 184; SU 189199).

Another of the Rockbourne group, this is the second largest long barrow in Hampshire. It is 320 feet (97 metres) long by 46 feet (14 metres) wide. The width has probably been reduced by the ploughing which has destroyed the side ditches.

BRONZE AGE

Although Hampshire does not present the wealth of bronze age communal monuments which is found, for instance, in Wiltshire and Dorset, detailed field work has collected considerable evidence for the so-called 'Wessex Culture' of the earlier bronze age (about 2100-1500 BC). There are over a thousand bowl barrows in the county although most have been considerably reduced by ploughing. Nineteen disc barrows have been listed as well as over thirty bell barrows.

Flower Down Disc Barrow, Littleton, Winchester (OS 185; SU 459319). At the southern end of Littleton behind the bus shelter.

The central mound of this barrow is over 98 feet (30 metres) across and is surrounded by a 20 foot (6 metre) wide ditch with a 180 foot (55 metre) diameter. Outside there is an outer bank of some 20 feet (6 metres) in width. There is a second mound slightly to the south-west.

Martin Down Enclosure, Martin (OS 184; SU 043201).

Although there must have been many bronze age occupation sites, very few have been identified. This enclosure was excavated by General Pitt-Rivers, who demonstrated that it was a bronze age cattle enclosure. It was surrounded by a V-shaped ditch with an internal bank which is just discernible today.

Petersfield Heath Barrow Cemetery, Petersfield (OS 197; SU 758232).

The barrows cover an extensive area, largely on a golf course. The group contains fifteen bowl barrows, four saucer barrows, a disc barrow and a bell barrow. Many of the monuments are obscured by the turf of the golf course while others are covered by woodland.

Roundwood Barrow Cemetery, Laverstoke (OS 185; SU 507444). Reached via a minor road north of the A303 close to its junction with the A30 near Micheldever Station.

There are four barrows in the group, some of which were excavated in 1920. The group is now much damaged by ploughing.

Seven Barrows, Burghclere (OS 185; SU 463555). Just west of A34 north of Litchfield.

This group of about nine barrows forms a line running north-south and is clearly visible from the A34. To the west of the A34 is a bell barrow standing about 7 feet (2 metres) high and four bowl barrows to the north of this, one of them now visible only from the air.

Stockbridge Down Round Barrow, Stockbridge (OS 185; SU 375347). On the north side of the A272.

This is a group of about sixteen barrows on National Trust land. They are small (less than 40 feet or 12 metres in diameter) and are largely degraded. One was excavated immediately prior to the Second World War.

Whiteshoot Plantation Barrows, Broughton (OS 185; SU 290329). On Broughton Down between Whiteshoot Plantation and a line of trees to the south.

There are three barrows in this group, a bell barrow and two saucer barrows. The saucer barrows are good examples of the type.

IRON AGE

There is a considerable body of archaeological evidence which has built up a comprehensive picture of society in iron age southern Britain, with its villages, field and farms. However, it was the hillforts, the urban centres which were the product of the gradual centralisation of power in the centuries before the Roman conquest, which remain as impressive monuments for the visitor to enjoy.

Beacon Hill, Kingsclere (OS 174; SU 458573). Telephone: 0962 64221. Hampshire County Council.

This dramatic hillfort lies at a height of 842 feet (257 metres) above sea level in Watership Down country. The climb up the hill from the car park at the bottom is hard work but is rewarded with spectacular views across the north of Hampshire. The fort is univallate with a single in-turned entrance and aerial photography has revealed a number of hut platforms within.

Butser Hill, Queen Elizabeth Country Park, Horndean. Hampshire County Council.

Butser Hill is a clay-capped plateau of 80 acres (32 ha) with traces of a complex of dykes of the late bronze age and iron age. The main ridge to the west is cut off by a bivallate cross-ridge dyke running parallel to a promontory dyke. This is generally considered to be an unfinished hillfort. Three other spurs of the hill are cut off by lines of entrenchment and it is thought that at least one of these forms a division between cultivated and uncultivated pastureland.

The north-east spur of the hill, called Little Butser, is the site of the Butser Ancient Farm

Excavations at Danebury iron age hillfort.

Project. The demonstration area, open to the public, is beside the A3, 3 miles (5 km) south of Petersfield; telephone: 0705 598838.

Bury Hill, Upper Clatford (OS 185; SU 345535).
This fort was excavated by Christopher Hawkes in 1939. It encloses about 22 acres (9 ha) and the earliest phase is represented by a univallate bank and ditch slightly offset from the later, and much stronger, bivallate fortifications. The entrance is on the south-east. Occupation continued into the Roman period.

Castle Ditches Hillfort, Whitsbury (OS 184; SU 128196).
In the west of the county, this hillfort looks down over the river Avon. It encloses about 15 acres (6 ha) with a double bank and ditch, the inner bank rising an impressive 20 feet (6 metres) above the original ground surface. Excavations have established that the fort was first constructed in the early iron age, although the top of the hill had been used as the junction point of bronze age boundary ditches. Occupation continued throughout the pre-Roman iron age. The fort appears to have been refurbished during the troubled years of the sixth or seventh centuries AD.

Danebury Hillfort, Nether Wallop (OS 185; SU 323377). Telephone: 0962 846034. Hampshire County Council.
This remarkable multivallate hillfort has been the subject of many seasons of archaeological excavation and should be visited in conjunction with the Museum of the Iron Age at Andover (see chapter 8). The excavations have been carried out in advance of a tree-planting operation to replace the beech trees planted in the nineteenth century. The work has provided the most comprehensive picture of the organisation and economy of a hillfort ever obtained.
The first defended settlement on Danebury was in existence by the middle of the sixth century BC. Some time about 400 BC the hillfort was extensively remodelled: the rampart heightened, the ditch re-dug and the two gates reconstructed. The defences were maintained in good order over the subsequent three hundred years but, although various improvements were made, they were not enough to prevent the eventual catastrophe which resulted in the burning of the east gate and the departure of most of the inhabitants around 100 BC.
The County Council has arranged a signposted walk around the 13 acre (5 ha) site, with magnificent views over the surrounding landscape.

Ladle Hill, Sydmonton (OS 174; SU 478568).
Approached by means of a bridleway to the east of the site.
This is one of the most interesting hillforts in the county in that it appears to be in an unfinished state. It has been suggested that it was originally a stock enclosure and that the sections of discontinuous ditch are part of preparations to turn it into a fully fledged

CHAPTER 3

hillfort. The fort occupies a prominent position looking across to Beacon Hill.

Old Winchester Hill, Meonstoke (OS 185; SU 641206).
This is a univallate contour hillfort with fine views over the Isle of Wight. The enclosure is about 14 acres (6 ha) with entrances at the east and west. Outside the ditch on the southern side are three mounds incorporated into the outer bank, possibly the remains of bronze age barrows cut by the construction of the fort. There are four bowl barrows on the crest inside the fort and six more outside the western end.

Quarley Hill, Quarley (OS 184; SU 262423).
Approached from the south along the road linking Grateley and the B3084.
The fort is a univallate enclosure with entrances at the north-west and south-east (although these may just be places where the fortifications were never finished). It was excavated in 1938 by Christopher Hawkes, who showed that the hill was first enclosed by a stockade in the early iron age. The fort is of special interest in that it overlies an extensive system of early boundary ditches which radiate from the hill.

St Catherine's Hill, Winchester (OS 185; SU 484276). Reached by a path on the south-west slope which rises from a car park on the south-bound carriageway of the Winchester bypass.
The hill, with its clump of trees at the summit, is a Winchester landmark. The fort is a contour type with a single rampart and outer ditch with a discontinuous counter-scarp bank dated to the second century BC. The defences make maximum use of the steep slope of the hill. Excavations by Christopher Hawkes uncovered a four-phase sequence at the gateway, ending in a fire in the first century BC. In the twelfth century a chapel dedicated to St Catherine was built on the hill, and there is a maze, reputedly cut in the turf by boys of Winchester College in the eighteenth century.

ROMAN
Hampshire was the heart of the prosperous, agricultural lowlands of Roman Britain. The archaeology of Roman Hampshire is as rich as it is varied, whether it is that of the Roman towns or of the villa economy in the countryside.
At the centre of the county is Winchester, founded on the site of a large late iron age enclosure in the first century AD and called *Venta Belgarum*, the capital of the administrative region of the *Civitas Belgarum*. In the second century, the town was entirely enclosed by a walled circuit, which was refurbished in

the tenth century and maintained throughout the middle ages. *Calleva Atrebatum*, in the north of the county, is known by its modern name of Silchester. Here the Roman town was abandoned and survives under the shallow soil. There is a third Roman town in the county, *Clausentum*, now known as Bitterne Manor, on the east bank of the river Itchen in Southampton.
Although Hampshire possesses few of the Roman military sites that characterise the north of Britain, it does have what must be the most complete Roman monument north of the Alps, the Saxon Shore fort of Portchester.
Rural archaeology, with its roads, villas, farmsteads and fields, is more difficult to present to the visitor. However, one excavated villa, at Rockbourne in the New Forest, is laid out with a small museum, while there are plans to display and interpret the villa excavated at Sparsholt near the Farley Mount Country Park (see chapter 2).

Portchester Castle. Telephone: 0705 378291. English Heritage.
Portchester Castle occupies a prominent position on the west side of Portsmouth Harbour. The circuit of the Roman walls, which enclose a square 610 by 620 feet (186 by 189 metres), is complete and contains a number of D-shaped bastions designed for artillery. The castle was probably built as a Saxon Shore fort during the troubled 280s when Carausius was appointed to command the Roman fleet with orders to clear the Channel of barbarian pirates. After the Carausian episode the fort was abandoned by the military although it appears to have been recommissioned during the 340s.
Excavations have provided details of the military occupation of the fort and its subsequent use by a civilian population well into the Saxon period. In the tenth century Portchester was one of the burghs listed in the Burghal Hidage and, to the north of the castle, there is evidence of a bank and ditch belonging to this period. During the reign of Henry I the Roman fortress was transformed into a medieval castle by the building of a keep and an inner bailey within the Roman walls, which then functioned as an outer bailey for the new castle (see chapter 5).

Rockbourne Villa, Rockbourne. Telephone: 07253 541 and 445. Hampshire County Council.
This villa was discovered before the Second World War and was excavated over a number of seasons by the owner of the land. The site was first established during the iron age; during the Roman period it developed into a villa with over fifty rooms around three sides of a courtyard. The excavations also unco-

14

The iron age hillfort on St Catherine's Hill, Winchester.

vered a separate bath-house as well as numerous farm buildings.

Much of the villa is uncovered, with the excavated walls, floors and rooms laid out for the visitor to see. During the summer two mosaic floors have their protective covers removed so that they too can be viewed. Near the excavated remains there is a small site museum with displays of the objects found.

Silchester (*Calleva Atrebatum*). Telephone: Silchester Museum 0734 700362.

Calleva Atrebatum was the capital city of the administrative area of Roman Britain known as the *Civitas Atrebatum*. The Roman town was built upon the site of a large pre-Roman settlement. The so-called outer earthwork, constructed during the reign of Cogidubnus, can be seen in Wall Lane, near Rye House (OS 175; SU 636628) or at Rampier Copse on the Wellington Estate. During the second century the area enclosed by the outer earthwork was reduced and a bank and ditch constructed along the line of the later town wall. The wall was constructed during the third century and, in places, rose to a height of over 22 feet (7 metres). There were four main gates, as well as three small posterns, but nothing remains to be seen of the east and west gates. The north gate can be seen from Wall Lane (OS 175; SU 638627) and the south gate, with the best preserved stretch of wall, can be seen near the church of St Mary.

The streets and buildings of Silchester lie buried beneath the fields which cover the entire interior of the walled circuit. From the air they appear as distinct crop marks. Silchester has been almost totally excavated by archaeologists between 1890 and the present day and it is possible to reconstruct the layout of the town with its houses, baths, temples, the forum with its basilica and the amphitheatre.

There is a small site museum at the village of Silchester but the best displays on the Roman town are to be found at Reading Museum.

Southampton (*Clausentum*). (OS 196; SU 420120).

Clausentum was probably established as a military supply base during the campaign to quell the Durotriges after the Claudian conquest. The peninsula of Bitterne Manor is formed by a bend of the river Itchen and this appears to have been fortified with cross dykes, later replaced by a wall. Excavations have taken place over the years and a small bath-house is exposed in the private grounds of Bitterne Manor. The explorer will find traces of the bank at the end of the aptly named Vespasian Road.

Winchester (*Venta Belgarum*).

Venta Belgarum was the administrative capital of the *Civitas Belgarum*. It was established in the first century, partly overlying a late iron age enclosure. Although the circuit of Roman walls was completely integrated into the late medieval defences, some of the Roman structures can be seen at Scott Garden overlooking the river Itchen, and the Roman bank can be seen behind the wall at the Pilgrim School playing fields near Wolvesey Castle.

15

4
Churches, cathedrals and abbeys

Andover: St Mary.
This, one of the great Victorian churches in Hampshire, was started in 1840 and dedicated four years later. It is Early English in its style and is an impressive sight on the hill overlooking the old town. The interior of the church is quite outstanding; the high plaster rib-vaults of the nave, the tall piers and the elegant tower arch create a visual *tour de force*.

Avington: St Mary.
Finished in 1771, this is one of the most perfect Georgian churches in the county. It is a short walk from Avington Park which is now open to the public (see chapter 6). The church is brick-built and has a tower with battlements, a feature which is carried along the length of the nave. The interior has a fine three-decker pulpit and is complete with box pews and the family pew belonging to Avington Park.

Beaulieu: Blessed Virgin and Child.
This church is of particular interest as it is the former refectory of Beaulieu Abbey (see chapter 6). The building dates from about 1230 but was made into the parish church after the

The Saxon doorway, Breamore church.

Dissolution. Although the original reading pulpit is gone, the stairs which led up to it survive. One monument of note in the churchyard is the gravestone of Michael Silver, master carpenter on HMS *Agamemnon*, the ship on which Nelson lost his eye.

Boarhunt: St Nicholas.
Boarhunt church lies to the north of Portsmouth, separated from the coast by the ridge of Portsdown Hill. The church lies in rural seclusion, the key being available from a nearby cottage. It is an almost complete Saxon church of the eleventh century. The nave and chancel are free from any later additions but the only surviving Saxon window is in the north wall of the chancel. The principal feature of the interior is the Saxon chancel arch decorated with a square-section raised band of stone running along the outside of the arch on its west face.

Bramley: St James.
The wall paintings are of special significance. There is a thirteenth-century depiction of the murder of Becket which has lost little of its vigour over the intervening centuries. Opposite there is a large fifteenth-century St Christopher. The chancel is decorated with more thirteenth-century paintings: masonry patterns, flowers and spirals together with a St James and a Virgin and Child. The window glass is exceptional and includes fourteenth-century pieces with figures of musicians and other characters.

Breamore: St Mary.
Situated near Breamore House (see chapter 6) and Countryside Museum (see chapter 8), the church of St Mary at Breamore in the New Forest is described by Pevsner as 'by far the most important and interesting Anglo-Saxon monument in Hampshire'. On architectural grounds its date would be about AD 1000; the overall plan is transitional between Anglo-Saxon and Romanesque, with its cruciform arrangement, but with chancel and transepts of Anglo-Saxon proportions.
Of particular interest is the south transept, which survives complete and is reached from the tower crossing by a narrow semicircular arch carrying the inscription HER SPUTELAD SEO GECPYDRAED NEC DE ('Here the covenant is explained to thee'). Above the south doorway, in the porch, is a monumental Saxon rood, carved in relief but hacked off flush with the wall by iconoclasts of a later generation. Despite its mutilation, the carving of Christ in agony, with his arms raised like wings, remains

16

East Wellow church and Florence Nightingale's grave.

one of the most powerful pieces of Anglo-Saxon sculpture in southern Britain.

Burghclere: Sandham Memorial Chapel. Telephone: 063527 394. National Trust.

The chapel was built for the Behrend family of Burghclere to allow Stanley Spencer to work on a set of murals which he had proposed. These were to be a war memorial and a memorial to Lieutenant Henry Sandham (brother of Mrs Behrend), who died while fighting in Macedonia. Stanley Spencer worked on the mural paintings between 1927 and 1932, basing them on sketches he had made just after the First World War. There are nineteen paintings, including the 'Resurrection of the Dead Soldiers' on the east wall and scenes depicting aspects of army life such as kit inspection, bed-making, the arrival of a convoy of wounded at the hospital, tea in a hospital ward and a dug-out at Salonika. The chapel is not only a monument, it is one of the major pieces of twentieth-century British art.

Corhampton

A few miles up the Meon valley from Boarhunt is the Saxon church of Corhampton. Sited on a raised 'island' above the surrounding fields, the church displays all the features of late Saxon work: the long-and-short quoins and, on the north, a blocked doorway with plain blocks instead of capitals and a pilaster strip running around the archway. Inside is a chancel arch decorated with a similar pilaster

strip while, on the south side, near the porch, is a Saxon sundial.

Crondall: All Saints.

Apart from the varied and interesting interior, which is mainly Norman and thirteenth-century Early English, and the fine Norman doorways, the most interesting feature is the seventeenth-century brick tower, which was built in 1659 at the cost of £428 to replace the medieval crossing tower which had to be dismantled. One item of note is Hampshire's oldest brass, a monument to Nicholas de Kaerment who was rector between 1361 and 1381.

Deane: All Saints.

This has been described as the most complete and successful early nineteenth-century Gothic church in the county. It was built in 1818 by an unknown architect. The church is famous for its plate and the remarkable Deane Cup, a tazza of 1551 now in the collection of the Hampshire County Museum Service.

Droxford: St Mary and All Saints.

A village church can tell the story of a community over many generations. This is the case at Droxford where there is a Norman nave and chancel arch together with work of the thirteenth, fourteenth and fifteenth centuries, a tower dated 1599, Georgian alterations and Victorian restorations.

17

East Meon: All Saints.
All Saints is tucked in under the hills of the South Downs, a cruciform church surmounted by a fine Romanesque tower. The west doorway is Norman, with zigzag ornamentation and fluted capitals. Inside the church is one of the famous Tournai marble fonts dating from the twelfth century. There are eight of these in Britain, four of them in Hampshire.

East Wellow: St Margaret.
Florence Nightingale lived at nearby Embley Park and is buried at East Wellow. The church dates mainly from the thirteenth century and is quite plain. Its most remarkable features are the wall paintings which include ashlar patterns decorated with rosettes. There is a painted St Christopher carrying the Child in his arms and, on the south chancel wall, the murder of Thomas à Becket.

Eversley: St Mary.
This is one of Hampshire's fine crop of Georgian churches. It is built of brick and carries the dates 1724 over the porch and 1753 on the tower. It was possibly designed by the local John James. Perhaps the best known association is that of Charles Kingsley, author of *The Water Babies,* who was curate here from 1834 to 1875.

Fareham: St Peter and St Paul.
The chief ornament of this church, which is an amalgam of medieval, Georgian, Victorian and twentieth-century work by Sir Charles Nicholson, is the fine brick north tower added in 1742.

Gosport: Holy Trinity.
This seventeenth-century church was completely remodelled by the Victorian architect Blomfield in 1887 and clad in mathematical tiles. Outside, the main feature is the brick campanile, a major Gosport landmark. Inside, the visitor is surprised to find the interior of 1696 largely intact. The nave piers are Ionic in form and are made of great tree trunks. The marble and mosaic high altar is the work of the Hampshire Arts and Crafts movement artist Heywood Sumner. The organ was originally in the private chapel of the Duke of Chandos at Stanmore in Middlesex; it was used by Handel when he was organist to the Duke.

Hannington: All Saints.
The little village of Hannington lies on the highest part of the Hampshire Downs in the north of the county, not far from Kingsclere. All Saints is one of a number of Hampshire churches in which the evidence of Saxon architecture is obscured by later accretions and is noticed only by the more observant visitor. The diagnostic long-and-short work of the

Saxon masons survives in the north-east quoin of the nave. Of particular interest is a Saxon sundial, discovered during restoration work in 1970 built into the south wall of the south aisle.

Headbourne Worthy: St Swithun.
Like Breamore, the church of St Swithun at Headbourne Worthy contains one of the great pieces of Anglo-Saxon art in southern Britain. The church is situated in a most delightful setting, with a tributary of the river Itchen flowing round the church, isolating the graveyard, with its springy lawns and fine trees, on a small island. Above the door at the west end of the church is a rood, a group of Christ on the cross, the Virgin and St John the Baptist. The figure of Christ resembles that of the Romsey rood, with the hand of God appearing out of a cloud. As with the rood at Breamore, iconoclasts have hacked the figures so that silhouettes are all that remain, but the power of the original carvings has survived to impress the visitor today.

Hound: St Mary.
There is not much more to Hound than its little church. It is a small church, with a simple nave and chancel and a weatherboarded bell turret at the west end. It has changed little since the thirteenth century and is memorable for its coherent simplicity.

Hursley: All Saints.
The church was built in 1846-8 and was paid for by John Keble, the pioneer of the Oxford Movement, who was vicar here. For the student of ecclesiology it is a must. The windows are to a design by William Butterfield.

Idsworth: St Hubert.
What makes this church special is not the magnificent Georgian interior with its gallery and box pews (which escaped Victorian restoration), although these are splendid enough, but the remarkable series of wall paintings which have been dated to about 1330. A series in the chancel is thought to represent the life of St Hubert; it includes hunting scenes with a white horse, hounds and a huntsman. There is a saintly figure together with an armed knight and a monster, which are taken to depict events from the saint's life. Other paintings show events in the life and death of John the Baptist. They are the most important medieval paintings in the county, all the more remarkable considering the fact that they are found in a humble village church.

Little Somborne: All Saints.
All Saints comprises a nave and chancel in one. The nave is Saxon, as can be seen by the fragments of pilaster strip on both north and south walls, work typical of tenth-century

Wessex. At the west end are long-and-short quoins, again typical of a tenth- or early eleventh-century date.

Lyndhurst: St Michael.
The church, designed by William White, was built between 1868 and 1870, its red-brick structure standing on a hill overlooking the picturesque High Street. The exposed brickwork of the interior, red, white and yellow, is dramatic in its effect. The reredos is painted by the Pre-Raphaelite Lord Leighton. The east window, representing the New Jerusalem, and the south transept window were designed by Sir Edward Burne-Jones for Morris and Company and are amongst the finest windows produced by that firm.
The clock in the tower was made by T. Cooke and Sons of York and installed in 1868. It is one of the best examples of this maker's work and is widely regarded as a national horological treasure. In the churchyard there is the grave of Mrs Reginald Hargreaves, born as Alice Liddell and immortalised as Lewis Carroll's *Alice in Wonderland.*

Mattingley
Perhaps the most remarkable and unusual feature of this late medieval church is that it is timber-framed throughout. The aisles were constructed in 1867 although the arcade piers are the wall posts of the original outer walls.

Micheldever: St Mary.
This church is of many periods. The medieval nave and chancel had a sixteenth-century west tower added, and then, in 1808, George Dance inserted a brick octagon in the centre. The chancel is of 1880-1. Members of the great Baring family of bankers are commemorated in three monuments by Flaxman of between 1801 and 1813.

Milford-on-Sea: All Saints.
Milford-on-Sea is generally associated with twentieth-century seaside housing development but it boasts one of the finest Early English medieval churches in Hampshire. There is evidence for an earlier Norman church, which may have had a crossing tower replaced by the present west tower before the middle of the thirteenth century. The thirteenth-century reconstruction included the building of aisles which took in the width of the original transepts.

Minstead: All Saints.
The church sits on a little hill overlooking the village and the surrounding New Forest. The Georgian interior is complete and unspoiled: box pews, a three-decker pulpit, galleries to increase the accommodation and an eighteenth-century addition to the west

gallery. There are two extraordinary family pews, fitted like small rooms, with separate entrances and one complete with its own fireplace.
The church, almost domestic and cottagelike with its dormer windows, looks over a churchyard which contains the grave of Sir Arthur Conan Doyle, creator of Sherlock Holmes, who lived at Minstead. There is also an interesting gravestone which carries a carving of a serpent; it is the memorial to an eighteenth-century musician who played this type of wind instrument, perhaps in the church band.

Netley Abbey, near Southampton. Telephone: 0703 453076. English Heritage.
Netley Abbey was a Cistercian foundation established by the monks of Beaulieu in 1239. The survival of the buildings after the Dissolution was due to Sir William Paulet converting the church and cloister buildings into a large dwelling. Today most of the mansion has long gone, leaving the medieval structures exposed. The ruined abbey played a great part in the eighteenth-century romantic movement. In the 1770s part of the north transept was removed to form a sham ruin in the grounds of Cranbury Park near Winchester.
The romantic ivy and trailing trees have

The grave of Conan Doyle at Minstead.

The twelfth-century Cistercian abbey at Netley.

been removed but Netley Abbey still recalls the pleasant associations of the romantics. There are substantial remains of both the church and the claustral buildings. The chapter house, parlour, subvault of the dorter, dorter and reredorter can all be traced and, in some cases, survive remarkably complete. The stone-lined garderobe, which was flushed by a stream, is a prominent feature of the reredorter, built over the monastic infirmary.

Petersfield: St Peter.

The exterior gives little clue to the existence of such a splendid interior. The church was started about 1120 with an ambitious plan for a central crossing tower which was never completed. The church was finished to a more modest plan towards the end of the twelfth century when a west tower was added. Most of this work survives so St Peter's is one of the most interesting Norman churches in the county. However, Blomfield did some restoration in the 1870s and much of the detail of the chancel dates from this period.

Portchester: St Mary.

St Mary's church is situated in the middle of the Roman fort. It is an outstanding and virtually complete Romanesque church, precisely dated as it was founded by Henry I in 1133 as an Augustinian priory. The west doorway is of three orders, with roll mouldings

and horizontal zigzag and relief circles decorating the arches. The shafts have incised spiral decoration. Another elaborate door, surmounted by a high pediment, presumably intended for the King and his retinue, is in the middle of the north wall, though this is largely obliterated. The eastern arm of the church has been reduced and the south transept demolished.

Portsmouth: Cathedral Church of St Thomas of Canterbury.

The church of St Thomas has been a cathedral only since 1927. It is, without doubt, the most eclectic combination of styles that could be imagined. The first church was founded about 1180 by a rich merchant, John de Gisors, and was built by the canons of Southwick Priory. The central tower was damaged in the Civil War and was rebuilt with the nave between 1683 and 1693. The church was considerably enlarged and modified in 1938-9, the old tower becoming the focal point of the new cathedral. The result is a muddled effect, not helped by the fact that the westward extension has never been finished.

The medieval work is now restricted to the choir and transepts and it is clear that the original church was ambitiously conceived. It belonged to the important period of transition between Romanesque and Early English, like the church of St Cross, Winchester. The nave of the medieval church was entirely replaced in the seventeenth century in a style reminiscent of the contemporary work by Wren in London. However, the seventeenth-century aisles were lost in the construction of much wider aisles during the twentieth-century extension. The seventeenth-century tower is surmounted by a wooden cupola which now carries a weather vane, a replica of one placed there in 1710 but blown down in a gale in 1954.

Portsmouth: Royal Garrison Church.

This was originally part of God's House, or the Hospital of St John and St Nicholas, founded at the beginning of the thirteenth century. After the Dissolution, the hospital buildings were converted into military stores and, later, a residence for the military governor of Portsmouth. Catherine of Braganza stayed here while awaiting the arrival of Charles II, whom she married in the church.

The church was bombed in the Second World War. The chancel, complete with its vaults, and which is still used by the congregation, dates from 1212-20. The nave, which is preserved roofless and is now separated from the chancel by a glazed screen, is somewhat later. The whole was thoroughly restored by G. E. Street in 1866.

Portsmouth: St Agatha.

There are many Victorian churches in Portsmouth but this is the most unusual. From the outside its brick-built basilica style is bleak, but it was never intended to be seen, as the church was crammed into a space between the slum housing of Landport. Inside it is the decoration which makes the church oustanding: Heywood Sumner created a great mosaic for the now demolished Lady Chapel, and he decorated the apse and dome with sgraffito scenes including a great Christ in Majesty. There is now a strong movement to preserve what is generally recognised as an art treasure of national significance.

Romsey Abbey

The first church at Romsey was part of the nunnery founded in AD 907 by Edward the Elder for his daughter Elfrida. This church was rebuilt in 967; the apse of this structure was exposed by archaeological excavations below the crossing of the present church, which was built between 1120 and about 1230. On entering from the north doorway the visitor is struck by the Romanesque grandeur of the building with its massive pillars and rounded arches. The first two bays of the nave are separated by a massive round pier that rises through the arcade into the gallery, after which the second pier is compound and a new scheme was developed. Four bays of the nave are Norman; the last three are Early English.

The two outstanding monuments at Romsey Abbey are both Anglo-Saxon. The remarkable rood that decorates the west wall of the south transept is of a figure of Christ standing 6 feet 9 inches (2 metres) high but, while being in the

The Royal Garrison Church, Portsmouth.

Romsey Abbey.

same tradition of the Hampshire roods at Breamore and Headbourne Worthy, the Romsey rood probably belongs to the years after the Norman conquest. Above the head of Christ is the hand of God emerging from a cloud. The characteristics of the modelling suggest an eleventh-century Ottonian influence.

Inside the abbey, in the south chancel, is a much smaller piece of tenth- or eleventh-century Anglo-Saxon sculpture of Christ crucified with two angels on the arms of the cross, the Virgin and St John below and Longinus the soldier, with the sponge, lower still.

Rotherwick

This church is noted for its fine timber-work and remarkable for the fact that the tower arch and the chancel arch are of wood. The whole church was originally timber-framed and received its present brick facing in the sixteenth century. The brick tower is one of the many fine seventeenth-century church towers in Hampshire.

St Mary Bourne: St Peter.

One of the four famous Hampshire fonts of Tournai marble is in St Peter's church (the others are at Southampton, East Meon and Winchester Cathedral). The church was first built in the twelfth century and much of the late Norman work survives. The subsequent architectural history of the church takes some

unravelling as it was altered throughout the middle ages. It is a perfect English village church in an idyllic setting.

Southampton: St Michael.

Situated in the heart of the old town in St Michael's Square, this is the oldest surviving church in the city: the other medieval churches were lost or damaged during the blitz of 1940. All that remains of the Norman church is the tall crossing arches, a dramatic survival from the days when Southampton and its merchants grew rich on trade with Angevin France. The fine black font of Tournai marble also dates from these days, when wealthy endowments were commonplace.

The church has been rebuilt and enlarged on several occasions; aisles were added in the late twelfth century when the chancel was altered. Both aisles and transepts were enlarged in the fifteenth century to encompass the original transepts, and the church was substantially rebuilt in 1828-9. At this time cast iron piers were inserted and the aisles were heightened to accommodate galleries. The medieval church did not have a spire; the first one was built as a navigation mark in 1732, the present spire being a rebuild of 1877.

Southwick: St James.

Like Minstead, Southwick is notable for the survival of its pre-Victorian interior. Despite the loss of the box pews in the nave in the

1950s, the surviving box pews, the three-decker pulpit and the galleries give the church an unspoilt Georgian appearance. There is a remarkable eighteenth-century reredos with balusters and paintings of cherubs. The church was rebuilt in 1566, a date recorded on a tablet on the external face of the east wall of the chancel.

Titchfield Abbey, Titchfield, Fareham PO15 5RA. Telephone: 0329 443016. English Heritage.

Titchfield Abbey is a Premonstratensian foundation established by Peter de Roches, Bishop of Winchester, in 1232. Little remains of the medieval buildings which were converted into a mansion after the Dissolution by Thomas Wriothesley, Earl of Southampton, whose grandson was patron to William Shakespeare. (There is a tradition that the first performance of *Romeo and Juliet* took place in the nearby tithe barn at Fern Hill Farm.) The principal remains are the magnificent Tudor gatehouse fashioned out of the abbey nave and designed in that peculiar 'Tudor Gothic' which characterised the gradual introduction of Renaissance ideas into England. Mock medievalism is evident in the arrow slits in the ground floor of the turrets which can never have been intended for defence.

The Titchfield tithe barn, a timber structure of the fifteenth century, is south-west of the abbey. It is 150 feet (46 metres) long and 40 feet (12 metres) wide, one of the most important late medieval agricultural buildings in the county.

Titchfield: St Peter.

The tower of St Peter at Titchfield is perhaps the most archaeologically significant Anglo-Saxon building in Hampshire. It is the only church known to have pre-Danish masonry surviving above ground and is now known to have been founded as a minster church in the seventh century as part of a deliberate act of policy by the Kings of Wessex. The surviving architectural evidence suggests that it was an impressive building, probably put up as part of a royal programme of assimilation of the area into the sphere of influence of the Saxon kings.

The lower part of the tower was built as a porch: such west porches were a common feature of seventh-century churches in Kent as well as in northern churches such as Monkwearmouth. A single-splay window in the west gable of the nave is again similar to the windows of late seventh- and early eighth-century Northumbria. The architectural similarities of the porch with Northumbrian churches suggest that it was built at the time of St Wilfrid's missionary work in Sussex (681-6).

Warblington: St Thomas à Becket.

This is one of the most picturesque churches in Hampshire in a delightful setting. There was a Saxon church here, probably with a two-storey western tower as at Titchfield. The upper stages of this tower survive in the crossing tower of the late twelfth or early thirteenth century. Outside, the church is covered by roofs which sweep down over the aisles almost to the ground.

The graveyard includes a number of fascinating eighteenth-century gravestones: one shows a fish swallowing a man drowned at sea; another has a man drowning in a ship turned upside down; a third shows HMS *Torbay* on fire in Portsmouth Dockyard in 1758. Two flint and brick huts survive in corners of the graveyard. They are gravewatchers' huts from the days when new graves had to be guarded against the grisly activities of body snatchers.

Warnford: Our Lady.

There are two inscriptions: one records that the church was founded by Wilfrid, the other that it was renovated by Adam de Port. Little remains of the Saxon church other than a sundial. The tower is Norman while the nave and chancel are Early English. The de Ports

St Michael's church, Southampton.

were amongst the greatest lay landlords in Hampshire by the time that Domesday was written. They not only had the manor house at Warnford but also the manor of Basing.

Whitchurch: All Hallows.
Of interest to any student of Anglo-Saxon art and architecture is a ninth-century gravestone in the Victorian church of All Hallows, Whitchurch. The stone has an arched top and, on the front, which is like that of a Roman legionary gravestone, there is an arched recess in which there is a figure, perhaps that of Christ. An inscription runs along the top in Roman letters: HIC CORPUS FRITHBURGAH REQUIESCIT IN PACE SEPULTUM. The back is decorated with a plain but well executed scroll.

Winchester: Cathedral Church of the Holy Trinity, St Peter, St Paul and St Swithun.

The three minsters
Throughout the Saxon period, Winchester retained its pre-eminence as an ecclesiastical centre. The first church founded in Winchester was established during the reign of King Cenwalh in or about AD 648. The church, dedicated to St Peter and St Paul, became the Old Minster and was the first building on the site of what is now Winchester Cathedral.

Excavations to the north of the present cathedral have shown that the original church was a cruciform structure with a north-south porticus opening off the nave, and an eastern arm, perhaps apsidal.

In 971 a massive rebuilding operation took place. The work involved the creation of the monastic precinct and the extensive remodelling of both the east and the west ends of the church. The building was extended westward over the site of the tomb of St Swithun to form one of the most imposing pieces of architecture in Anglo-Saxon England. The west end, which was finished about 980, and which towered up to 150 feet (46 metres) above the surrounding town, was the most impressive part of the 200 foot (61 metre) long church. The ground plan of the Old Minster has now been laid out in the turf to the north of the Norman cathedral.

In 903, the New Minster was founded just to the north of the Old Minster. It was dedicated by Edward the Elder and a church, twice as large as the extended Old Minster and capable of holding a large congregation, was built. In the 980s, the New Minster matched the buildings of the Old Minster with a tower, apparently six storeys high and richly decorated at each level. The proximity of the two churches led to many difficulties; these included complaints that one choir could not

The Tudor mansion of Titchfield Abbey.

(Left) The west front of Winchester Cathedral. (Right) Portsmouth Cathedral.

sing without being interrupted by the other.

A third monastery, the Nunnaminster, was founded at the same time as the New Minster, traditionally by Ealswith, Alfred's queen, but endowed and consecrated by her son, Edward the Elder. The foundation was to the east of the New Minster on a site enclosed by the two arms of the modern Colebrook Street. Following archaeological excavations, parts of the Nunnaminster have been laid out near the Winchester Guildhall.

The cathedral

The cathedral has an external length of 556 feet (169 metres), making it the longest in England and in Europe. The present building was started in 1079 by Walkelin, the first Norman bishop. Demolishing the magnificent Old Minster, which was less than a hundred years old, he intended his new cathedral to be larger than any contemporary church in either England or Normandy, a fitting symbol of the power of the new political dynasty which had established its principal palace some few yards to the west of the Old Minster.

The architecture of the Norman builders is best seen in the crypt, transepts and crossing. The crypt survives remarkably complete with its short round piers supporting groined vaults. Inside the church, the massive round arches on

three levels (arcade, triforium and clerestory) are best appreciated in the transepts. This is what Pevsner has called the 'most complete statement in England of the Early Norman style'. The finest stonework is found in the masonry of the crossing arches which were rebuilt after Walkelin's tower collapsed in 1107. Little remains of Walkelin's chancel and nave for the visitor to see inside the church. Outside, recent archaeological excavations have revealed that the west end originally included a westwork of two massive towers.

The remodelling of the Norman nave was begun by Bishop Edington and was carried through to completion by William of Wykeham, one of the great churchmen of the middle ages. His work dates from the years following 1394 and was carried out under the aegis of William de Wynford, a master mason who had been clerk of works at Windsor Castle. A major feature of this work was the demolition of the Norman westwork and the creation of the present west front, which many think is a disappointing face to what was still the largest cathedral in Europe. The internal elevation was modified by the cutting back of the large Norman piers to create the Perpendicular-style mouldings.

The retrochoir and the Lady Chapel were started by Bishop de Lucy (died 1204) and

25

completed in the thirteenth century. The arcades of the chancel, with their Purbeck marble piers, date from the fourteenth century but the wooden vaulted roof, with a series of 91 coloured roof bosses depicting the sufferings of Christ, dates from about 1505 and forms part of the improvements carried out by Bishop Fox. Of all the many monuments in the cathedral, perhaps the most remarkable are the series of wooden tomb-chests of Anglo-Saxon kings, and that of the Norman king William Rufus, which are to be found in the chancel. Of the more recent memorials, that dedicated to Jane Austen is the object of many modern pilgrims' interest.

The Close

In 1541 the prior and monks of St Swithun were reconstituted as dean and chapter and most of the cloister was destroyed in 1563. The entrance to the chapter house survives, described by Pevsner as 'one of the mightiest pieces of Norman architecture in the land'. Most of the claustral buildings of the middle ages have gone but the present precinct includes a remarkable collection of buildings in one of the most delightful settings that can be imagined. Entering the precinct at the south-west corner of the cathedral one is first impressed by the row of buttresses built to support the collapsing cathedral between 1905 and 1912. On the far side of the lawn is the deanery, the rib-vaulted porch of which is approached through three pointed arches dating from the fourteenth-century. The only other house in the precinct which contains substantial medieval remains is number 10, The Close, which has a vaulted room of the thirteenth century. Number 1, The Close, was built in 1699; number 4, the Judges' Lodging, is late seventeenth-century as are numbers 5-8 in Dome Alley. The Pilgrims' Hall dates from the mid fourteenth century and is remarkable in having the earliest known hammerbeam roof in Britain. Near the southern gateway of the precinct, St Swithun's Gate, is a dramatic row of gabled houses with timber-framed upper floors dating from the fifteenth century. These are the so-called Cheyne Court and the Porter's Lodge.

Winchester: St Cross.

St Cross Hospital was founded in 1136 by Bishop Henry de Blois, one of the great churchmen/statesmen of the twelfth century, but the present buildings appear to be those erected by Cardinal Beaufort about 1445. Entering through the gateway, the visitor passes into the Outer Court, which contains the site of the Hundred Men's Hall as well as

the kitchen of the hospital. The main quadrangle is entered through a massive gateway similar to those at Winchester College and here travellers may receive the traditional wayfarers' dole, a small glass of beer and some bread. The north side of the quadrangle comprises the hall in which the brethren of the hospital took their meals. The hall is approached through a vaulted porch and is dominated inside by a high roof of arched braces up to high collar beams, the roof timbers standing on stone angels' busts.

The west range of the hospital comprises the brethren's lodgings; each house has four lodgings off a main staircase and is served by one main chimney, the row of these forming a distinctive feature of the building. The Brethren of St Cross still wear their gowns and hats and may be seen regularly in the village or in Winchester.

The church of St Cross is one of the most interesting in Hampshire; it was started in the late twelfth century and fully demonstrates the transition from Romanesque to Gothic architecture. The interior of the church was substantially restored in the 1860s by Butterfield and it is often difficult to tell what is original.

St Cross is situated on the water meadows of the river Itchen, with a view over towards St Catherine's Hill. It must be one of the most delightful places for a walk in the whole of England.

Wolverton: St Catherine.

This is the finest early Georgian church in the county. It was built in 1717, a brick facing being applied to an earlier medieval church. The inside belongs to the Baroque tradition and may have been designed by a student of Christopher Wren. The box pews, the pulpit and the reading desk all belong to the eighteenth-century rebuilding.

Yateley: St Peter.

It is surprising to find remains of a substantial stone-built Saxon church in the north-east of the county, known from the Domesday Book to have been the poorest and least populated part of Hampshire before the Norman conquest. The north wall of the nave has long been known as Saxon due to the presence of long-and-short work, but it was a disastrous fire in 1979 that provided the opportunity of examining the extent of the Saxon structure. The church, with its distinctive fifteenth-century timber-framed west tower (which miraculously survived the fire) is now rebuilt as a modern church and hall.

Calshot Castle.

5
Castles and fortifications

Calshot Castle, Calshot Spit. Telephone: 0703 892023. English Heritage.

In 1538 France and the Holy Roman Emperor signed a treaty against the fickle King Henry VIII and an invasion of England seemed inevitable. In response, Henry commissioned the construction of a series of fortifications to defend the whole of the south coast. A number of forts were built in 1539-40, including Calshot and Hurst Castles, which, together with two blockhouses at East and West Cowes, defended the western approaches to Southampton Water. Further castles were built at Netley and near Hamble to defend the approaches to Southampton. The Solent was also defended with castles at Southsea and, on the Isle of Wight, at Sandown and, at Yarmouth.

Calshot Castle was one of the smaller forts, consisting of a three-storey central tower, a concentric curtain wall and a stone-lined moat. The eight embrasures and eighteen gun ports were arranged in three main tiers.

The fort survives complete and has recently been refurbished by English Heritage. The main rooms in the central keep contain exhibitions which tell the story of Calshot's long history from the sixteenth century to its famous role as a flying boat station in the twentieth century. The spectacular views over Southampton Water are as memorable as Calshot Castle itself.

Fort Brockhurst, Elson, Gosport. Telephone: 0705 581059. English Heritage.

In 1853 Napoleon's nephew, Louis Napoleon, declared himself Emperor and assumed the title Napoleon III. British public opinion was convinced that, given the chance, the new Emperor would revenge his uncle's defeat at Waterloo and invade England. In 1858 William Armstrong manufactured a rifled, breech-loading gun that doubled the range of artillery; in the hands of the French, such guns could bombard the dockyard at Portsmouth from positions well out of the range of existing defences. These two developments led to a general fear that a French force might land in West Sussex and secure positions on Portsdown Hill from which it could shell Portsmouth. In February 1860 a Royal Commission recommended that four forts be built on Portsdown Hill and its flanks reaching from Chichester to Fareham, and that a further three should be built on the Gosport peninsula. Nicknamed 'Palmerston Follies' (after the

27

then prime minister), the new defences were never put to the test, but they probably helped keep the peace at a time of international tension.

Fort Brockhurst was started in 1858, two years before the Royal Commission reported on the Portsmouth defences. However, it incorporated all the latest ideas on artillery defence: it was designed to carry nineteen heavy guns on its main ramparts, with a further eight on each flank. A lower tier of guns in casemates on each flank provided cross-fire with the neighbouring forts of Elson and Rowner in the Gosport Advanced Line. At the rear of the fort is a circular keep, in the tradition of medieval fortresses. The whole fort is surrounded by a moat protected by projecting caponiers.

A large building in the middle of the parade ground houses an exhibition on the development of the fortifications around Portsmouth. Although it never saw action (apart from three casemates destroyed by a German bomb in the Second World War), the displays portray the cost in human life when similar forts were held at Verdun during the First World War.

Fort Cumberland, Portsmouth. Ministry of Defence.

This is perhaps the best example of eighteenth-century defensive architecture in Britain and ideally represents the history of the defence of the realm between the seventeenth-century defences of Portsmouth and the nineteenth-century forts of Brockhurst and Widley. It was built in 1746 by the Duke of

Cumberland to defend Langstone Harbour to the east of Portsmouth. The ramparts are faced externally with stone; the gun emplacements are in vaulted brick chambers covered with earth. Cumberland was one of the last forts built on the bastion principle, which was superseded by the polygonal defences of the nineteenth century.

Fort Nelson, Military Road, Fareham. Telephone: 0329 233734. Hampshire County Council.

The fort is another 'Palmerston Folly' and was built in the middle of the nineteenth century at the same time as Fort Widley. At present access is available only for guided parties but there are plans to use the fort as an outstation of the Royal Armouries at the Tower of London and to make it into the national museum of artillery.

Fort Widley, Portsdown Hill, Portsmouth. Telephone: 0705 827261. Portsmouth City Council.

One of the 'Palmerston Follies', Ford Widley is placed on the crown of Portsdown Hill overlooking Portsmouth. Extensive tunnels, hewn out of the chalk, run underground between the central magazine and the gun batteries. The gun emplacements face inland over a terrain that was cleared of all buildings and trees to form a firing ground. The keep (of last resort, as at Brockhurst) is a rectangular barrack block defended by its own moat.

Guided tours take visitors down the underground passages to the casemates, caponiers

Fort Brockhurst, Gosport.

The Roman walls and towers of Portchester Castle.

and bastions of the fort. A climb on to the roof of the barrack building is rewarded with the finest possible view of Portsmouth and Spithead. The view at night is equally spectacular.

To the west of the fort stands the Nelson Monument, raised by Nelson's officers and men. The column is 120 feet (37 metres) high and contains a bust of the hero overlooking the harbour.

Hurst Castle. Telephone: 05904 2344. English Heritage.

Hurst Beach is a massive shingle spit protruding 2 miles (3 km) into the Solent from the New Forest coast. Here in 1541-4 Henry VIII built one of his castles as part of his plan to defend the Solent from French attack (see Calshot Castle). The castle can be approached either by a long walk along the beach or by boat (in summer) from Keyhaven.

At the centre of the castle is a twelve-sided keep surrounded by a nine-sided polygon fortified with three squat, semi-circular bastions. As with other Solent defences, Hurst Castle was strengthened with the addition of two massive flanking artillery bastions in 1861-73. These comprised 61 massive granite-faced casemates. The views across the Solent to the National Trust land overlooking the Needles are magnificent.

Portchester Castle, near Fareham. Telephone: 0705 378291. English Heritage.

The Roman remains of Portchester are described in chapter 3. The medieval castle was built in the north-west corner of the Roman fort, the walls of which formed the enclosure for the medieval outer bailey. The castle was built in the latter part of the reign of Henry I (1100-35) when a stone keep, surrounded by a bailey, was constructed. The keep was raised to its present height some time before 1175. The Roman walls were refurbished and the gateways rebuilt in twelfth-century style. Henry I made Portsmouth his usual point of departure for Normandy and, no doubt, the castle was built to facilitate this.

Little remains of the twelfth-century buildings within the inner bailey as Richard II built himself a small palace here between 1396 and 1399 (see chapter 6).

The castle was sold by the crown in 1632 but on several occasions it was rented back to provide accommodation for prisoners of war. Throughout the wars of the eighteenth century the castle was used as a large military prison for French captives. Many of the walls are cut with the names of Frenchmen incarcerated at Portchester.

Portsmouth town defences. Telephone: 0705 826722 for details of guided walks.

The strategic importance of Portsmouth in the defence of the realm makes it a unique site for the history of town defences in Britain. The surviving defences range in date from the early fifteenth century to the nineteenth-century forts on Portsdown Hill.

Old Portsmouth was entirely surrounded by artillery defences comprising stone curtain walls with angled bastions, facing moats with defensive ravelins. The landward defences are

29

Portsmouth fortifications from the sea.

largely gone (although the Landport Gate survives) but the seaward defences are substantially complete and make a pleasant promenade between the Point and Southsea.

The Round Tower stands by the shore on the harbour side of the Point at Old Portsmouth. The tower was first built in 1415 to defend the entrance to Portsmouth Harbour; much of the upper work dates from improvements made by Henry VIII between 1538 and 1540. The defences were later improved by Charles II under the supervision of Sir Bernard de Gomme, and the Eighteen Gun Battery, running south-west of the Round Tower, was built at this time. De Gomme also built the Flanking Battery at right angles and backing on to the Round Tower. The Eighteen Gun Battery was remodelled between 1847 and 1850 and now forms part of a splendid promenade from the Round Tower to the King's Bastion.

The next feature is the Square Tower, originally built in 1494 by Henry VII, and, for a century, the governors of the military garrison lived here. The tower was turned into a magazine in the late sixteenth century and was remodelled during the reconstruction of the town defences in the 1840s. It is soon to be opened as a museum. Running south from the Square Tower is the Ten Gun Battery, again originating in the sixteenth century, improved by de Gomme in the seventeenth century and raised in level in 1860. At the most southerly point of the town defences is the King's Bastion, the only extant example of the angle bastions which provided artillery protection along the landward side of the defences. Before this there is the Long Curtain, the only stretch of de Gomme's seventeenth-century work surviving in anything like its original form.

Southampton Castle, Southampton. Telephone: 0703 221106.

Although there might have been a Norman motte in Southampton, the first mention of a castle occurs in 1153. It was at that time that Southampton became important in the trade between England and Angevin France and the castle became a royal facility for the importing of wine, having its own quay and warehouses. Two quayside buildings survive from this first phase of the castle's history. There is a first-floor hall built between 1100 and 1150, the upper floor being royal apartments, the lower floor warehousing with direct access to the quay. Castle Vault, just to the north, was constructed about 1193. It is an impressive barrel-vaulted stone structure, the ribs resting on sixteen decorated corbels. In 1252 a new garderobe tower was built for the queen, and the fine stone-lined cesspit has now been excavated. It was of the very highest quality and was designed to be flushed by the rise and fall of the tide.

By 1270, the north of the castle had been

30

enclosed by a new wall and ditch (the wall being a prominent feature of the town today). The arches of the wall are, in fact, foundations that were originally covered by an earthen bank. In the fourteenth century a new defensive wall was built along the base of the cliff to the west, incorporating the walls of the earlier domestic buildings into the defences.

The castle was completely renovated between 1378 and 1388, and two of the castle gateways of this period, the Watergate and the foundations of the Eastgate, can still be seen. Nothing remains of the stone keep which was incorporated into a Gothic 'folly', Lansdowne Castle, built in 1804, and demolished in 1818.

Southampton town defences and gateways. Telephone: 0703 221106 for details of guided walks.

Southampton has the most extensive, and the most interesting, medieval town defences in Britain, other than those of York and Chester. Three of the original gateways survive, along with most of the northern stretch of walls, and the western walls with their distinctive arcade. The defences were largely completed in the decades following the French raid of 1338 and are of particular interest in having been designed with the introduction of artillery in mind.

The Bargate, which controlled access to the medieval town from the north, is the oldest building still in use in Southampton. The earliest parts date from the twelfth century,

but it was remodelled in the late fourteenth century with the addition of twin drum towers to the north and a large hall, later the town's Guildhall, was built over the gateway. The north face, with its heavy machicolations and defensive appearance, contrasts with the domestic appearance of the south face, which dates from the fifteenth century.

To the east of Bargate, the town wall is largely complete up to Polymond Tower at the north-east corner of the medieval town. To the west, it is interrupted by the intrusion of the modern Castle Way. From Arundel Tower at the north-east corner of the defences, the town wall runs without interruption to the southernmost point of the medieval castle. Built against a cliff, which was a feature of the medieval topography, the top of the walls is at a considerable height above the land reclaimed from the river Test.

To the south of the castle, the town wall incorporates within its structure the walls of massive stone-built merchants' houses dating from the twelfth century. One such, King John's House (see chapter 6), survives with all walls complete up to eaves height. The devastating French raid of 1338 led to the completion of the wall, which incorporated the quayside walls of the houses. Windows and doors were blocked up and keyhole gunports inserted to provide a comprehensive field of fire over the West Quay. Today, the ghosts of the blocked doors and arches make it possible to reconstruct the arrangement of houses

The Landport Gate, Portsmouth.

31

before the catastrophe of the raid.

To the south of West Quay is the Westgate, dating mainly from the early years of the fourteenth century. It was through this gateway that Henry V led his troops to embark on the expedition that was to lead to the victory at Agincourt. The gateway also saw the departure of the Pilgrim Fathers on their historic voyage to America on 15th August 1620. The development of Town Quay at the beginning of the nineteenth century was responsible for the loss of most of the southern stretch of the walls. However, at the south-east corner of the town remains the gateway built by the medieval hospital of God's House, together with one of the most remarkable medieval defensive buildings in Britain.

God's House Tower was built in the first decades of the fifteenth century as an artillery battery to protect Town Quay and the eastern defences of the town. It is the earliest purpose-built residential gun tower in Europe. The tower, with three levels of guns, is linked to the town walls by a gallery which had gunports above a vaulted magazine.

The eastern town walls run north from God's House for about one-third of their original length. They include a tower that was built in the fourteenth century on the foundations of a stone dovecote of the twelfth century. The medieval friary lay to the north, and the walls incorporate a gateway built by the friary for its own use, as well as the Friars' Garite or watchtower built in 1371.

Southsea Castle, Portsmouth PO5 3PA. Telephone: 0705 827261. Portsmouth City Council.

Southsea Castle was completed by 1544 as part of the coastal defences constructed by Henry VIII to counter the threat of invasion from France (see Calshot Castle). In its original form it comprised a square keep inside a square enceinte set diamond-fashion to the keep and with flanking gun platforms. The square form is in contrast to the round keeps of the contemporary Solent forts. The keep survives much as Henry VIII built it and it now houses a museum of Portsmouth local history (see chapter 8). Despite reconstruction by de Gomme in 1683, the Henrican enceinte, with its gun platforms, is still there. In 1814 it was enlarged to the north to provide accommodation for the garrison and in the 1860s the whole castle was again enlarged with massive ramparts along the sea front. The castle remained in military occupation until 1960 when it was acquired by Portsmouth Corporation.

Spit Bank Fort, Portsmouth. Telephone: 0705 502551.

The so-called 'Palmerston Follies', which were built to defend Portsmouth in the middle of the nineteenth century, included a number of giant sea forts placed near the shipping lanes. Spit Bank Fort lies near the main deep-water channel into Portsmouth and was started in 1862. The fort is a massive structure of granite and Portland stone, some 50 yards (46 metres) in diameter. The walls are up to 15 feet (5 metres) thick and contain a maze of passages. Visitors can explore the fort, the magazines (with the special containers for oil lights), the gun emplacements and the accommodation for the complement of over 150 men.

Boats regularly leave for the fort from Clarence Pier, Southsea, from Gosport Hard and from the Isle of Wight.

Winchester Castle and Great Hall, Winchester. Telephone: 0962 841841.

William the Conqueror ordered the construction of a new castle at Winchester barely two months after his victory at Hastings. The castle was built in the south-west corner of the town defences; some fifty houses and two streets were demolished to make way for the Norman earthworks. At this time the castle was purely military, the royal residence being at a new palace lying between the cathedral and the High Street.

The castle defences were transformed by Henry III, whose work included the replacement of the great square keep with a round tower equipped with sally-ports. The foundations of the tower are now laid out in the Castle Yard near the present Castle Hall, also built by Henry III between 1222 and 1236. The total cost of Henry's work, which established the final form of the medieval castle, was over £10,000. He was a frequent visitor to Winchester and spent eighteen Christmases in the city.

Throughout its life, the castle withstood several sieges but the medieval structures were unable to withstand the bombardment by Cromwell's guns in September and October 1645. Six years later the walls and towers were demolished so that they could never again pose a threat to the Commonwealth.

The Great Hall of Winchester Castle is the finest surviving aisled hall of the thirteenth century. It is 111 feet (34 metres) long and 55 feet (17 metres) wide. It has undergone at least one major reconstruction (1348-9) when the aisle walls were heightened. Throughout most of its life the hall has been used for holding courts of law.

Recent analysis of the famous Round Table in the Great Hall has suggested that it was made in the period 1250-80, during the latter years of the reign of Henry III or the early part of the reign of Edward I. The latter was known to have had a special interest in the romances of the Arthurian cycle. The painting on the table is known to have been made in 1522 for the visit of the Holy Roman Emperor, Charles

Kingsgate, Winchester.

V of Spain. The figure of Arthur was painted to depict the young Henry VIII, who wished to impress his Imperial visitor with his own ancient lineage. It would seem that the table was not painted when it was first put up in the thirteenth century.

Through a doorway on the south side of the hall is a re-creation of a medieval castle garden named Queen Eleanor's Garden (see chapter 6).

Winchester Westgate and defences. Telephone: 0962 68166 extension 269.

The line of the walls of Winchester was established during the Roman period when *Venta Belgarum* was the market centre for the administrative area of the *Civitas Belgarum*. The Saxon document, the Burghal Hidage, makes it clear that the defences of the Saxon burgh incorporated the Roman walls, which survived into the medieval period. Most of the city walls were demolished in the eighteenth and nineteenth centuries but an extensive stretch survives up to its full height at the south-east part of the city, around the walls of Wolvesey Castle. At the Pilgrim School playing fields, the ramp of earth piled up behind the walls is part of the original Roman structure. At the eastern end of the city, near the lower part of the High Street, a fragment of Roman wall excavated in 1951 is preserved on view behind a grating in a modern wall bounding The Weirs at Scott Garden.

The Westgate is one of two surviving gateways; most of the present structure dates from the twelfth to the fourteenth centuries although it incorporates a few stones of the gateway to the Saxon town. The west wall was entirely rebuilt in the fourteenth century when a portcullis, machicolations, gunports and, possibly, a drawbridge were added. The inverted key gunports were intended for breech-loading hand cannons and, with those at Southampton, are amongst the earliest pieces of architectural evidence for the use of artillery in Britain.

The medieval Kingsgate, a charming gateway which houses the Hampshire Bookshop and, above, the church of St Swithun-upon-Kingsgate, links the Winchester College area with the cathedral precinct.

Wolvesey Castle, Winchester. Telephone: 0962 54766. English Heritage.

The creation of a separate palace for the Bishop of Winchester appears to date from the reforms of Aethelwold in the tenth century. A large stone hall was constructed on the site at the beginning of the twelfth century. It was an episcopal residence built on a grand scale and continued to function as such until the seventeenth century. In the 1140s Bishop Henry de Blois used material from the old royal palace (destroyed in the fighting of the civil war), to build new accommodation and to fortify his palace at Wolvesey where he could carry out his functions as brother to the king, papal legate and Bishop of Winchester. Both the new and the old buildings were enclosed by a defensive wall, the construction of which was followed by the erection of a large keep-like structure.

Wolvesey suffered the same fate as Winchester Castle after the civil war of the seventeenth century and was deliberately demolished. The present bishop's residence was then built from one wing by Bishop Morley, the work starting in 1684.

33

Broadlands House, Romsey.

6
Historic houses and gardens

Alresford House, Old Alresford. Telephone: 096273 2843.

This red-brick house was built about 1752 by Sir George Brydges Rodney — the famous Admiral Lord Rodney — who made his money capturing ships during the War of the Austrian Succession, thereby restoring the family fortunes lost in the South Sea Bubble. A cannon captured by the Admiral in an action against the French in 1782 still stands on the terrace at the house. In 1939 the house was purchased by the distinguished fighter pilot Gerald Maxwell, who built a small Catholic chapel which is decorated with a *trompe l'oeil* by Pietro Annigoni.

Avington Park, near Winchester. Telephone: 096278 202.

Avington Park has welcomed many famous guests including Nell Gwynne and Mrs Fitzherbert. The existing house dates mainly from 1705-15, the west front being dominated by a massive wooden portico comprising four Tuscan columns and a pediment based on St Paul's, Covent Garden. Guided tours take the visitor around the impressive ballroom with late seventeenth-century ceiling paintings, the library decorated with Pompeian wall paintings and the nineteenth-century conservatory, where teas are sold in the season.

Basing House, Old Basing, near Basingstoke. Telephone: 0256 467294. Hampshire County Council.

Basing House belonged to the greatest of Hampshire's Royalist supporters during the Civil War, William Paulet, Marquess of Winchester. His house was possibly the grandest Tudor house in England but all that remains are the banks, ditches and footings of walls which he turned into a stronghold that withstood the most famous siege of the Civil War.

There were two houses at Old Basing. The Old House was built in the 1530s on the site of a Norman castle. An illustration by Wenceslaus Hollar shows it to have had four or five towers, a Tudor version of its medieval forerunner. In one of the two baileys of the medieval castle was a second house, the New House. Cromwell's chaplain recorded his impression before the end of the siege: 'A nest of idolatry, the new house, surpassing the old house in beauty and stateliness, and either of them fit to make an Emperor's court...'

The siege of the house by seven thousand troops and over thirty cannon is one of the great stories of warfare, drama and heroism. The first attack came on 31st July 1643 when Colonel Richard Norton tried to take the house. The Royalist Lieutenant-Colonel Peake repulsed the attack and started to defend the house with earthworks. After almost continual siege, the eventual fall of Basing House did not come until October 1645.

The County Council has laid out the site with an explanatory exhibition in a Victorian lodge. As well as the remains of the castle and the house, there is a fine sixteenth-century dovecote and a magnificent sixteenth-century brick-built tithe barn. The Basingstoke Canal (chapter 7) was cut through the site of Old Basing and provides additional interest to a visit there.

Beaulieu Abbey, Beaulieu SO4 7ZN. Telephone: (0590) 612345.

Beaulieu Abbey was acquired by Sir Thomas Wriothesley at the time of the Dissolution, after which most of the monastic buildings were demolished. The refectory has survived as the present parish church (see chapter 4) and the fourteenth-century gatehouse has become the present Palace House, the home of the Montagu family since 1538. The house takes on much of its present form from a rebuilding in 'Scottish baronial' style by the first Lord Montagu of Beaulieu in the 1870s, under the direction of the architect Arthur Blomfield.

Although it is possible to visit the parish church of Beaulieu without paying, a visit to the rest of the abbey remains must be paid for at the entrance to the National Motor Museum (see chapter 8). The abbey was founded by the Cistercians in 1204, the church being completed in 1246. The ground plan of the church, of typical Cistercian form, is laid out for the visitor to see, but all that is left above ground is some of the south aisle wall and the doorway into the cloister. Much of the cloister survives, though the only complete building is the west range that contained the lay brothers' quarters. The frater and the adjoining cellarium now house a permanent exhibition about monastic life at Beaulieu, which was opened by Sir Arthur Bryant in 1977.

Bishop's Waltham Palace, Bishop's Waltham. Telephone: 04893 2460. English Heritage.

The twelfth-century Bishop of Winchester Henry de Blois built a number of castle-residences in Hampshire (see Wolvesey Castle in chapter 5). One of these was Bishop's Waltham Palace, first built about 1135 but destroyed when Henry II came to the throne. A major rebuilding took place between 1160 and 1180 when a palatial group of buildings

was erected. Henry II came here in 1182 and Henry V stayed in the palace en route to Agincourt in 1415. The palace was remodelled by Bishop Langton (1493-1501), when the red-brick wall which now surrounds the site was built. The palace was besieged shortly after the nearby battle of Cheriton in 1644 and was extensively damaged.

The visitor now enters through the remains of a gatehouse. The great hall of the palace was in the west range overlooking the surrounding moat towards the Winchester road. The kitchen was to the north of the hall and this connected with the twelfth-century tower in the south-west corner.

Bohunt Manor, Liphook. Telephone: 0428 722208.

This is a woodland garden with walks along a lake and water gardens. It is noted for its herbaceous borders, flowering shrubs and many rare species of trees. There are many types of waterfowl.

Breamore House, Breamore, near Fordingbridge SP6 2DF. Telephone: 0725 22270.

This fine Elizabethan manor house was built in 1583. Set in parkland in an unspoilt Tudor village, Breamore House contains magnificent collections of pictures, porcelain and furniture. It remains to this day the family home of the Hulses. Other attractions include the Countryside Museum (see chapter 8) and the Carriage Museum.

Broadlands House, Romsey. Telephone: 0794 516878.

Broadlands is famous as the home of Earl Mountbatten of Burma, whose life is commemorated in a large exhibition built in a converted stable block and opened by Prince Charles in 1981. The new exhibition includes a sophisticated audio-visual show that traces the life of Lord and Lady Mountbatten, two of the great public figures of the twentieth century.

There has been a house at Broadlands since the surrender of the land to Henry VIII by Romsey Abbey at the time of the Dissolution. In its present form the house dates mainly from the reconstruction by the second Viscount Palmerston in the years following 1767. The transformation of a Tudor manor house into a Palladian masterpiece was undertaken by 'Capability' Brown, followed by further alterations by Henry Holland in 1788. The western side, facing over the diverted river Test, is dominated by a giant portico with pediment.

On the first floor is the portico room, used by the Queen and Prince Philip on their honeymoon in 1947. In 1981, the Prince and Princess of Wales began their honeymoon at Broadlands.

Exbury Gardens.

Canute's Palace, Porter Lane, Southampton. Telephone: Tourist Information Centre 0703 221106. Southampton Tourist Guides Association.

At the lower end of the High Street in Porter Lane, Canute's Palace is one of two twelfth-century merchants' houses to survive largely intact in Southampton. It was damaged in the blitz of 1941 but enough remains to make an impressive ruin. Like King John's House, Southampton, it had a first-floor solar reached by a staircase that once protruded into the lane. The house is long and narrow and originally faced on to the Town Quay before the enclosure of the town in the fourteenth century.

Exbury Gardens, Exbury, near Southampton SO4 1AZ. Telephone: 0703 891203.

During the 1920s and the 1930s Lionel de Rothschild established one of the world's largest collections of rhododendrons in his 200 acre (81 ha) garden. The Exbury rhododendrons and azaleas are internationally famous and over 1200 hybrids have been created. The collection was developed in an oak wood and an arboretum, established by earlier owners of the estate. Great cedars and Wellingtonias create a marvellous setting for what is now recognised as one of the great woodland gardens of the British Isles.

58 French Street, Southampton. Telephone: 0892 48166. English Heritage.

Described as the most complete thirteenth-century merchant's house on its original site anywhere in Europe, 58 French Street has just been restored to its original condition. As with most Southampton town houses of the period, it is a three-bay timber construction over a stone-vaulted undercroft which had its own access and was let as a separate shop. The bay facing French Street has been restored as a shop with wooden shutters and has a chamber above. The central bay is open to the roof and has a restored fireplace against the north wall. The rear bay, again of two floors, has a chamber above and a parlour on the ground floor. The building has been furnished with reconstructions of the furniture that would have been found in a house of this period.

The Grange, Northington. Telephone: 0892 48166. English Heritage. The Grange is 8 miles (13 km) north-east of Winchester and 4 miles (6 km) north of New Alresford off the B3086.

This is the most important neo-classical country house in Europe and one of the great preservationist *causes célèbres* of modern times. What survives is a shell built in the form of a Greek temple around a pre-existing seventeenth-century house, the interior of which has now been demolished. In 1804 The Grange was acquired by Henry Drummond, who commissioned William Wilkins to transform his house into a Grecian temple. This was achieved by encasing the ground floor within a platform upon which he built a magnificent Parthenon portico, six Doric columns wide and two deep. The banker Alexander Baring then purchased the house and added the Orangery, another monumental classical temple with a delicate Ionic portico facing the cast iron and glass structure.

Highclere Castle, Highclere, near Newbury RG15 9RN. Telephone: 0635 253210.

Highclere is the largest mansion in Hampshire, set in a landscape designed by 'Capability' Brown during 1774-7. The earlier house on the site was remodelled to form the present mansion by Charles Barry, architect of the Houses of Parliament. It was designed for the third Earl of Carnarvon and was built between 1839 and 1842. Much of the grand interior is by a later architect who worked for the fourth Earl. Of particular note is the Gothic-style Great Hall which measures 70 feet (21.3 metres) by 24 feet (7.3 metres). The fifth Earl, whose monument crowns the nearby iron age hillfort on Beacon Hill (see chapter 3), achieved fame for his part in discovering the tomb of Tutankhamun in 1922. There is an interesting Egyptology collection in the house.

The magnificent park, described by William Cobbett as 'the prettiest park that I have ever seen', contains a classical temple from Devonshire House in Piccadilly, a rotunda and a funeral chapel. Highclere Castle opened to the public for the first time in 1988.

Hillier's Arboretum, Jermyns Lane, Ampfield, near Romsey. Telephone: 0794 68787. Hampshire County Council.

Named after Sir Harold Hillier who established the largest collection of trees and shrubs in the temperate world, the Arboretum covers 160 acres (65 ha) and contains over 360,000 species and varieties of woody plants and others, including bulbs and herbaceous plants from every continent of the world. The collection is at its most impressive during April and May when the rhododendrons, magnolias, azaleas and cherries provide a glory of colours.

Many of the plants are rare, even in their native habitats, so the Arboretum plays an important role in conserving endangered species. It is also an important educational resource in the county.

Hinton Ampner near Alresford. Telephone: 096279 361. National Trust.

Hinton Ampner House itself has been rebuilt twice since 1930, most recently following a fire in 1960. The gardens are the creation of Sir Ralph Dutton, who started his work about 1935 and created an architectural garden of grassy walks, yew hedges and vistas leading up to climaxes of classical statues. In his record of the garden Dutton describes many features of

garden history including the vestiges of a Tudor garden, a terrace bowling green or 'troco' and Victorian gardens on the estate.

Hollycombe House, Hollycombe, near Liphook. Telephone: 0428 723233.

This is a 10 acre (4 ha) woodland garden with large areas of rhododendrons and azaleas.

Houghton Lodge, Stockbridge SO20 6LQ. Telephone: 0264 810502.

This is an eighteenth-century *cottage orné* in Gothic style with fine views over the river Test. Rare cob walls enclose a traditional large kitchen garden and there are extensive glasshouses with a vinery.

Jane Austen's House, Chawton, near Alton GU34 1SD. Telephone: 0420 83262. At the corner of the old Winchester and Fareham roads.

Although she is more often associated with Bath, Jane Austen was a Hampshire Austen. She spent the first 25 years of her life at Steventon, near Basingstoke, and she lived in Southampton between 1807 and 1809, when she moved to the house at Chawton. Jane Austen lived here until a few weeks before her death in Winchester on 18th July 1817, and it was at Chawton that she completed most of her major works. The house is a modest

The thirteenth-century merchant's house at 58 French Street, Southampton.

37

The Grange, Northington.

seventeenth-century brick dwelling and is now open as a Jane Austen museum.

Visiting Jane Austen's house is more than visiting a museum: it is an experience that brings the visitor close to one of the greatest writers in the English language.

King John's House, St Michael's Square, Southampton. Telephone: 0703 332513. Southampton City Council.

Situated in the garden of Tudor House Museum (see chapter 8), King John's House was built in the twelfth century when Southampton grew rich on the trade between England and Angevin France. The Southampton merchants built stone houses which were equal to any baronial hall. The house comprises a first-floor hall over a warehouse which had direct access on to the West Quay. The two-light, round-headed windows of the solar survive at first-floor level together with a fine fireplace. At ground-floor level the doorways and windows that looked over the quay were blocked when the house was incorporated into the town defences after the French raid of 1338 (see chapter 5). Gunports were inserted into two of the window openings to form part of a battery designed to protect the quay.

King John's House, Warnford. Just outside the modern village, approached through Warnford Park.

King John's House, Warnford, was built in the late twelfth or early thirteenth century as an aisled hall of three bays. The stone piers were originally 25 feet (8 metres) high. The house is a rare example in Hampshire of a rural, stone-built hall house. It was one of the secondary residences of the de Port family which had become one of the great Hampshire landlords by the time of Domesday. The house is situated in the delightful Meon valley.

Leigh Park Gardens and Sir George Staunton Estate, Havant. Telephone: 0705 451540. Portsmouth City Council.

George Thomas Staunton settled at Leigh Park about 1820 after a career with the Honourable East India Company. He set about creating a landscape garden in the great eighteenth-century tradition. Amongst the follies in the park are a Turkish Tent, a Corinthian Bridge, a Chinese Bridge and a Chinese Boat House. Staunton was also an eminent botanist and plant collector.

The house was demolished in the 1860s but much of the estate has survived and is now managed as a country park. As well as the landscaped gardens there are areas of forestry and stretches under cultivation. Rare breeds of farm animals and poultry are kept on the farmland and at the Home Farm of 1821.

38

Marsh Court, Stockbridge. Telephone: 0425 72348.

The house was designed by Sir Edwin Lutyens and the gardens by Gertrude Jekyll. Access is by appointment only.

Medieval Undercrofts, Southampton. Telephone: Tourist Information Centre 0703 221106. Southampton Tourist Guides Association.

Canute's Palace is one of a number of medieval structures that survive at the lower end of High Street and which have been exposed either by bombing or archaeological excavation. Two of the complete undercrofts can be visited in parties led by the tourist guides. Quilter's Vault is a long tunnel vault, half underground, approached by its original steps off High Street. Just to the north is the vault at 98 High Street, wholly underground and approached by a modern spiral staircase.

The Undercroft is the most architecturally distinguished of the Southampton vaults. It is a two-bay undercroft with quadripartite ribbed vaults decorated with corbels and bosses reminiscent of contemporary work at Winchester Cathedral. The Undercroft has a fine fourteenth-century fireplace which underlines its function as a shop as well as a warehouse.

Mottisfont Abbey, near Romsey. Telephone: 0794 40757. National Trust.

If one is to see the conversion of a medieval monastery into a post-Dissolution mansion then it is to Mottisfont (rather than Netley or Titchfield, where the mansions have now vanished) that the visitor should go. Here the nave of the Augustinian priory church, which was consecrated in 1224, was converted into a mansion by William Sandys (see also The Vyne) between 1536 and 1540.

The conversion was achieved by inserting a floor into the nave of the church and reducing the height of the tower. The nature of this transformation can still be appreciated on the north side of the house where the full length of the nave can be seen up to the tower, which still rises a little way above the roof line.

Less of the medieval fabric can be seen in the south front. Sandys utilised the conventual buildings of the friary to construct a conventional Tudor courtyard house, but the wings were truncated in the eighteenth century under the ownership of Sir Richard Mill. A friend of John Chute of The Vyne, it was he who adopted the romantic appellation 'Abbey' for the house. The north walk of the medieval cloister was turned into an internal passageway with a gallery above providing access to the upstairs rooms.

In 1934 the Barker-Mill family sold Mottisfont to Gilbert Russel, under whose ownership two of the glories of Mottisfont were created. These were the conversion of the former hall into a saloon, the ceiling and walls of which were painted by Rex Whistler in 1938-9, and the renaissance of the gardens. In the saloon, Whistler and his assistants created a Gothic

Jane Austen's House, Chawton.

trompe l'oeil of magnificent proportions.

The garden of Mottisfont is one of the most delightful in Hampshire and is regularly used in the summer for the staging of plays. A spring rises nearby and is channelled into the river Test; all about is a remarkable collection of trees. In front of the south face, on the site of the cloister garth, is a parterre planted by the Russels in 1938. In the walled garden is the National Trust's collection of historic roses planted in 1972-3. Also in the grounds there is a large ice house, one of the few that can be seen in Hampshire.

The Oates Memorial Library and Museum and Gilbert White Museum, The Wakes, Selborne, near Alton. Telephone: 042050 275.

Gilbert White, the famous naturalist curate of Selborne, lived at The Wakes (for the museum see chapter 8). White's garden reflects the eighteenth-century taste for the picturesque landscape and is one of the best documented gardens of the period. The garden includes the original ha-ha, a section of White's fruit wall, a wild garden, a water garden and a rose garden. There is also a herb garden and a bird hide.

Queen Eleanor's Garden, The Great Hall, Winchester. Telephone: 0962 54411 extension 569. Hampshire County Council.

This garden has been created out of a small patch of land tucked between the medieval Great Hall and the nineteenth-century Winchester Barracks. It is an accurate re-creation of a thirteenth-century castle pleasure garden and was opened by Her Majesty the Queen Mother on 8th July 1986. It incorporates a fountain, a tunnel arbour and a turf seat. In the summer sun, the smell of herbs, the red and white roses, the Madonna lilies and the white doves flying overhead create a haven in the middle of a busy modern city.

The Red Lion, High Street, Southampton.

When Jane Austen visited a friend in Southampton's High Street she described the house as being 'à la Southampton, three deep'. She was describing the conventional medieval town-house pattern of a three-bay house set with its narrow gable to the street frontage. One such house remains in Southampton High Street. This is the Red Lion public house, which has a two-floor front bay with a gabled attic, behind which is a massive and impressive hall, open to the roof and with a massive stone fireplace.

The Royal Palace, Portchester Castle, Portchester. Telephone: 0705 378291. English Heritage.

Portchester Castle has been described previously (see chapters 3 and 5). The palace was built by Richard II between 1396 and 1399 around the whole western part of the inner bailey of the castle. As with other houses of the period, the principal rooms were on the first floor, the lower floor in this case containing four separate lodgings for members of the household, each with its own front door.

Next to the gatehouse, the kitchen was open to the rafters, and from this room steps went up to the first floor and the buttery of the great hall. The main entrance to the hall is by a porch that projects into the courtyard. A door leads from the dais bay to the great chamber, a magnificent room with a large fireplace and lit by four large windows. The chamber itself led to an inner chamber or bedroom and to the exchequer chamber where the business of the royal household was dealt with.

St Leonard's Grange, Beaulieu, Brockenhurst SO42 7XF. Not open to the public.

One of the granges of the Cistercian monastery of Beaulieu, the east gable and part of the west gable survive to show what a huge and impressive structure this must have been. The barn was 227 feet (69 metres) long, 68 feet (21 metres) wide and 55 feet (17 metres) high. Its capacity was more than half a million cubic feet (15,000 cubic metres). A model of the barn, one-tenth actual size, is on display in the Beaulieu Abbey museum.

Stansted Park, Rowlands Castle. Telephone: 0705 412265.

The home of the Earl and Countess of Bessborough, Stansted Park offers the visitor an elegant, unspoilt house set in glorious parkland. A small theatre museum displays costumes. Family portraits, a collection of bird paintings, tapestries, china and kitchen copper are on view. The grounds contain a unique chapel, arboretum and walled gardens.

Stratfield Saye House, near Basingstoke. Telephone: 0256 882882.

In 1817 Stratfield Saye House was given by a grateful nation to the Duke of Wellington, its saviour at the battle of Waterloo. The interest of the house is not in the architecture but in its association with the Iron Duke, one of the great soldier-statesmen of the nineteenth century.

Visitors may walk around the ground floor of the house and in the many rooms there are impressive collections of art treasures and the personal possessions of the first Duke. There is also an exhibition illustrating the Iron Duke's military career in India, the Peninsular campaigns and the battle of Waterloo, as well as his later public life in politics. On display are a number of items of clothing found

The Tudor Garden at Tudor House Museum, Southampton.

preserved in trunks at the Duke's London home, Apsley House. Another exhibition is built around the funeral hearse of the Iron Duke, made from guns captured at Waterloo; it weighs 18 tons and is 17 feet (5 metres) high and was pulled by twelve horses at the Iron Duke's funeral in 1852.

The Wellington Country Park is a nearby attraction which opened in 1974 (see chapter 9).

Tithe Barn, Titchfield.

Situated at Fern Hill near Titchfield Abbey (see chapter 4), this barn is one of the most impressive late medieval commercial buildings in Hampshire. It dates from the fifteenth century and is 150 feet (46 metres) long and 40 feet (12 metres) wide.

Tudor House Museum and Garden, St Michael's Square, Southampton. Telephone: 0703 224216. Southampton City Council.

Tudor House is one of the most remarkable late medieval houses in the county and also features the best researched reconstruction of

a Tudor garden in Britain. The architectural history of the house is complex and much remains to be unravelled. Although the building owes much of its present form to the work of Sir John Dawtrey, one of Southampton's rich merchant capitalists, who owned it between about 1490 and 1518, it incorporates a row of thirteenth-century houses. The very fine stone-vaulted undercroft of one of these survives in the basement. The wing of the house which faces on to Blue Anchor Lane appears to incorporate a further thirteenth-century house. The banqueting hall, which is set behind a three-storey range of chambers facing St Michael's Square, may have been originally open to the roof but had a wooden ceiling inserted either by Dawtrey or by Richard Lyster, Chief Justice of England, who married his widow. Tudor House is now one of the City Museums, with displays on social and local history (see chapter 8).

As with Queen Eleanor's Garden in Southampton, the designer of Tudor House Garden was Dr Sylvia Landsberg. There were several well-established features, such as a mulberry tree and a fig tree, before the garden was opened in 1982. It incorporates many features such as an arbour, rails and heraldic posts, raised beds and a knot garden. The wide range of plants and herbs have labels which explain their use in the sixteenth century. Beekeeping is practised here in Tudor style with straw hives kept on a thatched stand in a 'secret' garden, beside the main garden.

Tudor Merchant's Hall, Southampton. Southampton City Council.

The restoration of this building, which is situated adjacent to the medieval West Gate, established that it was originally built in the fourteenth century in St Michael's Square. Archaeology has demonstrated that it was placed diagonally across the square while documentary sources have indicated that there was the cloth market on the first floor and the fish market below. Examination of the building shows that it originally had an open arcaded timber ground floor.

By the 1630s the building was derelict and was sold by the Corporation to a local merchant who re-erected it on its present site, utilising the town wall to support one side and reconstructing the ground floor with a stone wall.

The Vyne, Sherborne St John, near Basingstoke. Telephone: 0256 881337. National Trust.

Hampshire's most famous country house was built between 1500 and 1520 by William Sandys, a member of an ancient Hampshire family whose rise to affluence and honour was due to long service under Henry VIII. Sandys became Lord Chamberlain and also obtained possession of Mottisfont Abbey.

In 1653 The Vyne was purchased by Chaloner Chute, a successful barrister who became Speaker of the House of Commons under Richard Cromwell. It was Sir Charles Chute, also a barrister, who bequeathed The Vyne to the National Trust in 1956.

In architectural terms the house reflects changing fashions over three hundred years. The south front still retains the E-plan and the mellow red brickwork of Sandys's house but the windows and the shallow, two-storey porch all date from the seventeenth century. The north side, facing the lawns that lead down to the impounded river Shir, is dominated by a portico built in 1654, the earliest example of a classical portico forming part of an English country house.

Visitors enter the house via the Stone Gallery which occupies the whole ground floor of the west wing, converted into a greenhouse in the eighteenth century. In the middle of the south front there is a classical staircase where there should be a Tudor one. Pevsner calls it 'the spatially most fascinating staircase composition of the second half of the eighteenth century in England'. It was designed by John Chute, a friend of Horace Walpole, who called it 'theatrical', a reaction common to most modern visitors.

Although some regard the staircase as the greatest glory of The Vyne, others will claim the title for the Oak Gallery, which extends for the entire length of the first floor of the west wing. It is panelled in the original intricate linen-fold panelling covered by the arms and devices of Sandys and his important contemporaries.

The chapel at The Vyne has been described as the best late medieval private chapel in England. It represents the gradual transition from high medieval into the Renaissance tradition. The windows of the chapel are, for the date, unequalled in Britain.

West Green House, Hartley Wintney. Telephone: 0372 53401. National Trust.

This is a charming house built in the early decades of the eighteenth century and now open on a restricted basis, together with a very fine garden.

The Wool House, Bugle Street, Southampton. Telephone: 0703 224216. Southampton City Council.

One of the most important medieval warehouses in the country, the Wool House was built at the beginning of the fifteenth century by the monks of Beaulieu for the storage of wool exported through Southampton. By 1407 the building was occupied by a leading burgess, Thomas Middleton, who financed the reconstruction of the Town Quay about this time. By the sixteenth century it was known as the Alum House, reflecting the importance of that commodity in the trade with Genoa.

The building was used as a prison during the wars of the eighteenth century and prisoners' names can be seen carved on the beams. The southern part of the building was reconstructed here when E. R. Moon used the building as a workshop and factory just before the First World War. The Wool House is now used as the Southampton Maritime Museum (see chapter 8).

Eastney Pumping Station, Portsmouth.

7
Industrial archaeology

Basingstoke Canal. Telephone: Canal Manager, Ash Lock, Aldershot, 0252 313810. Hampshire County Council.

The Basingstoke Canal was opened in 1784 to link Basingstoke with the river Wey and thence with London. It rarely lived up to the expectations of its promoters and, although a number of schemes emerged to link it with the Itchen Navigation and the Andover Canal, none of these passed the planning stage. The Hampshire section of the canal closed to traffic in 1906 and the western end has now disappeared. In recent years the cooperative effort of volunteers and local authorities has restored almost 30 miles (48 km) to both water craft and walkers.

A good place to start an exploration of the canal in Hampshire is Odiham, from where the towpath to North Warnborough is a public footpath. It was the collapse of the nearby Greywell Tunnel (SU 708518-719515) which sealed the commercial fate of the waterway but it has now been restored. The tunnel is a valuable home for numerous bats which can be seen flying out as evening falls. Colt Hill Bridge, to the east of Odiham, is a good base for walks or boat trips. Passing east, the canal goes through woodlands around Dogmersfield Park before crossing the heathland of Alder-

shot. Past Aldershot the canal crosses the Blackwater valley on a long embankment before descending through a series of locks which have now been restored.

Although much of the western end is lost, the canal can be explored near Basing (see chapter 6).

Botley Mill, Botley.

This mill is still in commercial production. The oldest surviving part, a three-storey brick building with a tiled roof, dates from 1770. The original wheels have gone and the stones are now powered by an Armfield turbine assisted by an electric motor.

Bursledon Windmill, Bursledon. Telephone: Friends of Bursledon Windmill 042121 3134. Hampshire Buildings Preservation Trust Ltd.

Built in 1813, this mill ceased working in the 1880s. Much of the original wooden machinery survived sufficiently for restoration or replacement to be undertaken. The mill is occasionally open as restoration proceeds; when this work is completed it will be used to grind corn once again. A staddlestone granary and a barn have been rescued from other sites and will be re-erected close to the windmill.

CHAPTER 7

Eastney Pumping Station, Eastney, Portsmouth. Telephone: 0705 827261. Portsmouth City Council.

The magnificently restored James Watt beam engines of 1886 at Eastney Pumping Station cannot fail to impress. The massive 23 foot (7 metre) long beams and the chapel-like interior of the pump house are testimony to the Victorian engineers and their knowledge that cleanliness is next to godliness.

Portsea Island is low lying and flat so a steam pumping engine was built at Eastney in 1868 to pump sewage into Langstone Harbour. Unfortunately the pumping had to take place whatever the state of the tide so the shore line around Eastney and Fort Cumberland became badly polluted. At times this was so bad that the barracks at Fort Cumberland had to be evacuated. The solution was the construction of giant storage tanks to be built at Fort Cumberland under an arrangement by which the Corporation would transfer equivalent land near Eastney Barracks to the military.

The present pump house, the 150 horsepower beam engines and the four Lancashire boilers date from a reconstruction of 1886. An adjacent building of 1904 houses a collection of Crossley gas engines.

Eling Tide Mill, The Causeway, Eling, near Southampton. Telephone: 0703 869575. Eling Tide Mill Trust Limited.

Tide mills work on the basis of a mill pond being filled at high tide, the impounded water then being allowed to fall through the mill during the period of low tide. Once tide mills were common, but Eling is the only mill of its type producing flour in Britain. The mill is at the head of Southampton Water where Bartley Water flows from the New Forest into the river Test.

There has been a mill at Eling for 900 years but the present mill building was built by Winchester College in the eighteenth century and continued working until after the Second World War. It was restored and opened in 1980 as a working mill building. Visitors to the mill can explore the machinery from the bin loft at the top to the wheels in the mill race. Demonstrations of milling are given several times a week and flour from the mill can be bought at the museum shop.

There are small museum displays on local history and the work of restoring the mill. Near the mill is Eling Quay which still accommodates commercial shipping, although yachts have largely replaced the sailing ships and barges that used to bring cargoes of wheat for the mill or barley for the local brewers.

Funtley Ironworks, Funtley, near Titchfield.

Funtley Ironworks has been described as one of the country's most important industrial archaeological sites. Whereas Coalbrookdale was the birthplace of the revolution in cast iron, Funtley was as important in the industrial production of wrought iron.

A forge, owned by the Earl of Southampton, operated here in the seventeenth century. Henry Cort took over the works in 1775 and experimented in puddling and rolling, which led to his famous patents of 1783 and 1784. The works operated well into the second half of the nineteenth century. There are the remains of a finery forge, a puddling furnace and housings for two wheels for driving rollers. The hammer pond and the waterwheel, which provided power for the site, can still be seen.

Itchen Navigation

It is possible to walk the entire length of the navigation from Northam Bridge in Southampton to Blackbridge Wharf in Winchester (see chapter 2). Starting from the Southampton end, and the much overgrown lock at Mansbridge, and walking along the towpath from here, the bed of the navigation is clearly seen, although it has now been drained. The next feature is Sandys Lock, again much overgrown. Conegar Lock (SU 466188), like the others, has turf sides, although the erosion of the sides of the chambers has been reduced by a brick toe.

The first road bridge above Mansbridge was at Bishopstoke where there is one of the iron span bridges built by the local Highways Board in the 1880s (SU 465193). For a short distance the Navigation then follows the main stream of the river until Withymead Lock, where a modern weir has replaced the gates. Allbrook Lock (SU 462212), a brick-sided structure, was reconstructed in 1838 and survives in good condition. The position of the top gates can be clearly seen. The waterway then travels along an embankment raised above the surrounding meadows for a short distance. At Shawford there were the single gates of a half lock (SU 474248) but care must be taken as the footpath which follows the towpath along much of this length is not always clearly defined.

There is a mill at Shawford and, from the junction with the millstream above Shawford Bridge, the navigation used the river rather than an artificial cut. The next feature is Twyford Lock (SU 476256) and then, passing more water meadows, there is the Twyford Lane End Lock before the footpath makes a significant diversion to cross the Winchester bypass.

Just before Winchester there is St Catherine's Hill Lock which is the summit of the navigation (SU 480274). In the latter part of the nineteenth century there was a water-driven saw-mill here. The pound above the summit lock has been used for many years by

Eling Tide Mill, near Southampton.

Winchester College for boating and from here the towpath is well defined up to Blackbridge, where the wharf marks the end of the navigation. Two survivals at Blackbridge are a warehouse and the former manager's house.

Mid-Hants Railway. Telephone: 096273 3810. Mid-Hants Railway PLC, Alresford Station, Alresford.

The Mid-Hants Railway is known locally as the Watercress Line. It runs over 10 miles (16 km) between Alresford and Alton through some of Hampshire's most beautiful countryside. The line closed in 1973 after an undistinguished history, following which it was bought by preservationists who have made it into one of the most successful preserved steam railways in Britain. It is possible to board trains at either Alton Station or Alresford Station and there are two intermediate stations, Medstead and Four Marks, and Ropley. At Ropley a variety of steam locomotives may be seen in various stages of restoration. There is a small museum in a railway coach at Alresford and a regular 'wine-and-dine' service on the 'Watercress Belle'.

The Salterns, Pennington, Lymington.

Salt production was one of the main extractive industries of Hampshire before the discov-
ery of rock salt in the late seventeenth century. Salt was extracted by impounding sea water in tidal ponds which were shallow and about 20 feet (6 metres) square. The water was then run into evaporating pans and left until it formed a strong brine. It was then pumped from the salterns by wind pump into boiling houses with coal-fired furnaces, where the water was driven off to leave salt crystals. The Chequers Inn, Pennington (SZ 323936), was the headquarters of the officials who collected the salt tax when the salterns were in production.

Southwick Brewhouse, High Street, Southwick, near Portsmouth. Telephone: 0705 380978.

This small traditional village brewhouse was built to serve an off-licence in Portsmouth and the nearby Golden Lion public house. It stopped brewing in 1956 but all the equipment, including the steam engine which drove the machinery, was left intact.

The brewhouse was restored by volunteers of the Southampton University Industrial Archaeology Group who carried out a commemorative brew of 300 gallons (1360 litres) in June 1985. Visitors can see the grist mill on the first floor used for cracking the barley, the mash tun in which it was soaked to allow its starch to be leached out, the barrel into which the resultant wort was fed, the boiling copper and the all-important fermenting casks.

Twyford Pumping Station, Twyford.
This water-pumping station was built by the South Hants Water Company in 1898 and a preservation trust has now been formed to ensure that the surviving building, with its 1910 triple expansion steam engine, and the adjacent bottle-shaped lime kilns are preserved. Occasional open days are organised.

Whitchurch Silk Mills, Winchester Street, Whitchurch. Telephone: 025689 3882. Hampshire Buildings Preservation Trust.
The elegant brick-built mill with its pediment and distinctive cupola dates from the

beginning of the nineteenth century. The mill wheel, which provided power for the mill, and much of the original machinery survive intact.
Built as a brush-making factory, the mill started manufacturing silk about 1830 and soon employed over a hundred workers. The traditional skills of winding the silk, warping and weaving the final cloth are fascinating to watch. Five hundred bobbins, each containing 12 miles (19 km) of thread, have to be prepared before the warp is set up on the loom. The mill produces material for legal silks, fashion clothes and a theatrical costumier.
The mill is open to the public and there is a shop on the premises where products of the mill can be purchased.

Buckler's Hard village.

8
Museums and art galleries

ALDERSHOT
Aldershot Military Museum and Heritage Centre, Queens Avenue, Aldershot. Telephone: 0252 314598. Aldershot Military Historical Trust.

Aldershot has been the home of the British Army since 1854 when 10,000 acres (4000 ha) of heathland were turned over to the military at the start of the Crimean War. The military town owes its origin to the convenient rail connection that made it possible to transport the masses of troops needed for the war to the waiting ships in Southampton docks. After the Crimean War, permanent buildings replaced the temporary wooden structures.

The Heritage Centre tells the story of military Aldershot with vivid modern displays which cover the growth of the camp, the origins of military aviation under Samuel F. Cody and, with the re-creation of a Victorian barrack room, the everyday life of the soldier in peacetime.

The Heritage Centre is an essential first step in the exploration of the military heritage of Aldershot, which includes many fine museums (listed below).

Airborne Forces Museum, Browning Barracks, Aldershot. Telephone: 0252 24431 extension 4619.

Army Physical Training Corps Museum, Queens Avenue, Aldershot. Telephone: 0252 24431 extension 2131.

Queen Alexandra's Royal Army Nursing Corps Museum, Farnborough Road, Aldershot. Telephone: 0252 24431 extension 4301/4315.

Royal Army Dental Corps Museum, Evelyn Woods Road, Aldershot. Telephone: 0252 24431 extension 3470.

Royal Army Veterinary Corps Museum, Galway Road, Aldershot. Telephone: 0252 24431 extension 2261.

Royal Corps of Transport Museum, Buller Barracks, Aldershot. Telephone: 0252 24431 extension 2417.

ALTON
Allen Gallery, Church Street, Alton. Hampshire County Museum Service.

The Allen Gallery contains extensive displays of the decorative arts, including English ceramics and oriental china dating back to the sixteenth century. The displays of silver include the famous Tichborne spoons which

were made in 1592 and presented to Sir Robert Tichborne, a Hampshire man who was then Lord Mayor of London.

Curtis Museum, High Street, Alton. Telephone: 0420 82802. Hampshire County Museum Service.

Named after William Curtis, the eighteenth-century botanist, the museum contains the county's displays of natural history and geology as well as exhibitions on local history. There is material on the local brewing industry and local history and archaeology, and also good collections on Victorian and later social history.

ANDOVER
Andover Museum and Art Gallery, Church Close, Andover. Telephone: 0264 66283. Hampshire County Museum Service.

Using the best of modern display techniques the story of life in and around the nearby hillfort of Danebury between 600 BC and AD 50 is recreated in a vivid manner in the Museum of the Iron Age. Themes include 'Aggression and Defence', 'Daily Bread' and 'Death and Burial'. Thousands of artefacts have been excavated over eighteen years and many are included in the displays. There are reconstructions of the ramparts of the hillfort, a round house of the type built within the fort, storage pits and one of the many graves.

The museum also features displays of local natural history and geology and local history, including the famous Tasker works which produced much of the agricultural machinery used in the county.

BASINGSTOKE
Willis Museum and Art Gallery, Old Town Hall, Basingstoke. Telephone: 0256 465902. Hampshire County Museum Service.

A major exhibition on the archaeology of Hampshire features the tusk of the woolly mammoth found near Odiham together with flint tools of late Pleistocene hunters.

Also of wide interest are the displays on natural history of North Hampshire which re-create many aspects of wild habitats with lifelike dioramas, and there is an aquarium of fish native to Hampshire.

The highlight of the museum is the collection of watches and clocks brought together by the museum's founder and first curator, George Willis. The collection ranges from the middle ages to modern times and includes an Act of Parliament clock named after a tax imposed by the government on clock owners in 1797.

CHAPTER 8

BEAULIEU

National Motor Museum, Beaulieu. Telephone: 0590 612345.

This is the county's largest museum and is amongst the top ten tourist attractions in Britain. Admission is to the National Motor Museum as well as to the Beaulieu Abbey ruins and Palace (see chapter 6). The collection was first brought together by Lord Montagu of Beaulieu and the museum is now the leading centre for the study of motoring history. 250 cars, commercial vehicles and motorcycles are on display, telling the story of motoring from 1894 to the present day. There are vintage cars, such as the 1899 Daimler 12 horsepower which belonged to John Scott-Montagu and which took Edward VII on some of his first motor rides. Sports cars, limousines, family saloons and racing cars are here in profusion. In pride of place are the record-breakers such as the 1929 *Golden Arrow* and Donald Campbell's *Bluebird* of 1961 which reached the speed of 403.1 mph (648.7 km/h).

'Wheels' is a ride-through display in which visitors, travelling in remotely controlled vehicles, are taken through exhibitions on the achievements of the motor car, including some fantasies as to what the future might bring.

BOTLEY

Hampshire Farm Museum, Manor Farm, Brook Lane, Botley SO3 2ER. Telephone: 04892 87055. Hampshire County Museum Service.

The Farm Museum is one of the most enjoyable of the many museums in Hampshire for a family outing. Passing through the entrance building with its audio-visual show, one immediately enters a farmyard complete with dung heap, chickens scratching in the yard, cattle, sheep, horses and pigs. The museum shows the development of agriculture in Hampshire between 1850 and 1950 and uses the buildings of Manor Farm, augmented by buildings that have been acquired and reconstructed, such as a staddle barn, a wheelwright's shop and a forge.

It is a living farm museum and historically significant breeds of animal are maintained, such as the black and white Wessex Saddleback pigs and Shorthorn cattle which used to be common in Hampshire. The museum's machinery is used to cultivate and harvest fields at the appropriate times of year. Demonstrations of farming and country pursuits, including baking and threshing, take place regularly.

The farmhouse reconstructs life around 1900 and the kitchen garden is maintained, growing the produce that would have supported the farming family throughout the year.

BREAMORE

Breamore Countryside Museum, Breamore, near Fordingbridge SP6 2DF. Telephone: 0725 22270.

The museum is built within a large walled garden of Breamore House (see chapter 6) and includes an extensive collection of tools and equipment used in field, farmyard, barn or workshop in bygone days. The collections are displayed to illustrate work on the farm in the different seasons of the year.

The museum includes a reconstruction of a blacksmith's forge and a wheelwright's shop as well as a dairy (with all the implements for producing butter, cream and cheese), a small brewery, a saddler's and a cobbler's. Another building contains a labourer's cottage, so faithfully reconstructed that it appears as if the inhabitants have gone out for a moment just as the visitor has walked through the door. The history of the tractor, a fundamental influence on the development of farming, is featured in a fine collection, including a Saunderson Mills of 1919.

BUCKLER'S HARD

Buckler's Hard and Maritime Museum, Buckler's Hard, near Beaulieu. Telephone: 059063 203.

In the 1720s a plan to build Montagu Town as a port to rival Southampton and to import sugar from the West Indies was put into effect. The main street was erected before the scheme foundered, and this survives today as Buckler's Hard.

The two rows of brick-built houses, reaching down towards the Beaulieu River, are unique. Despite the many thousands of visitors each year, the place retains an historical feeling and one can experience the atmosphere of the eighteenth century.

The village acquired importance as a centre for naval shipbuilding between 1745 and 1822. The greatest shipbuilder was Henry Adams, who completed his first ship in 1747 and launched Nelson's favourite ship, the *Agamemnon,* in 1781. Adams's two sons carried on the business until 1814. At the bottom of the High Street one can still make out the position of the building docks, while a remarkable model in the museum reconstructs how Buckler's Hard appeared at the height of its prosperity as a shipbuilding centre in 1803.

The museum tells the story of the village and its shipbuilding. Dramatic reconstructions, using life-size figures, show what life was like for rich and poor in Buckler's Hard during its heyday. One cottage, poor and threadbare, is shown as that of a simple labourer, James Bound; another is reconstructed as the more comfortable abode of Thomas Burlace, a skilled shipwright who lived in the village. Another displays the interior of the village inn,

48

Hampshire Farm Museum, Botley.

with the inhabitants playing cards around the fire. One curiosity in the museum is a set of baby clothes that belonged to Nelson.

EASTLEIGH
Eastleigh Museum, High Street, Eastleigh. Telephone: 0703 643026. Hampshire County Museum Service.

This museum was opened on 3rd October 1986 to mark the fiftieth anniversary of Eastleigh's status as a borough. There are displays of local history which reflect the growth of the town and the fortunes of its main industry, the railway works. A video projection area shows historic films of life in Eastleigh.

GOSPORT
Gosport Museum and Art Gallery, Walpole Road, Gosport. Telephone: 0705 588035. Gosport Borough Council.

Gosport's local museum contains well constructed and integrated displays which cover the geology of the area, archaeology from the palaeolithic to the medieval period, and more recent local history.

Naval Ordnance Museum, Priddy's Hard, Gosport. Telephone: 0705 822351 extension 44225.

As it is situated in the heart of a Royal Naval Armaments Depot, access to this museum is generally by appointment with the Curator. This remarkable and little known museum

deserves wider attention as it is one of the finest defence heritage collections in the south. Priddy's Hard was laid out about 1773 as a powder depot for the warships in Portsmouth Harbour, complete with magazine building and its little harbour for the powder hoys. It is the best example remaining in England. The museum is housed in the main magazine designed to store 4500 barrels of powder.

The displays tell the story of ordnance and its administration from its earliest days and include shot and shell of all types, together with many of the guns themselves. The torpedo collection is the largest in Britain and various sea mines, anti-submarine weapons, bombs and missiles are on display. There is a large archive collection, with material dating back to the seventeenth century, which is available for reference.

Royal Navy Submarine Museum and HMS Alliance, HMS *Dolphin,* Haslar Jetty Road, Gosport PO12 2AS. Telephone: 0705 529217.

HMS *Dolphin* has been a submarine base since the earliest days of underwater warfare. The first submarine with the Royal Navy was HM Submarine Torpedo Boat Number 1 (*Holland I*), built in 1901 to the designs of J. P. Holland and described by the Admiralty as a 'damned un-English' weapon. One of the remarkable feats of underwater archaeology has been the recovery of *Holland I* (which sank in 1913) and it is now a prime exhibit at the Submarine Museum.

49

The principal attraction is HMS *Alliance*, the last of the famous Second World War 'A' class boats, which has been lifted clear of the water on a massive cradle and is open to the public. The submarine had a range of 10,000 miles (16,000 km) and carried sixteen torpedoes fired through stern and bow torpedo tubes. The tubes and their complex mechanisms, the escape apparatus, the accommodation (with bunks shared between men on alternate watches), the control room with its two periscopes, the engine rooms and the motor rooms are all preserved in immaculate condition.

The extensive displays in the adjacent museum tell the story of submarine warfare from the days of the American Civil War to the nuclear-powered submarines of the modern navy. HMS *Alliance* and the museum are a formal memorial to the 4334 British submariners who died in two world wars and to the 734 officers and men lost in peacetime disasters.

HAVANT
Havant Museum and Art Gallery, East Street, Havant. Telephone: 0705 451155. Hampshire County Museum Service.

The finest aspect of this museum is the extensive and very well displayed collection of firearms donated by C. G. Vokes, who, amongst other things, invented the windscreen wiper. The collection includes a Winchester repeating rifle which belonged to Buffalo Bill. There is a fine display on wildfowling, which was a popular sport all along the Solent shores. There are also collections on the local history of the area.

LYNDHURST
New Forest Museum and Visitor Centre, The Car Park, Lyndhurst. Telephone: 0590 612047.

Lyndhurst is at the heart of the New Forest and the easily accessible visitor centre is an ideal introduction to any visit. Exhibitions and a multi-projector audio-visual show introduce the forest, with its long and varied history and natural history. The visitor can find out how the forest came into existence and learn about the traditions and customs and the people who live and work in it. The centre includes a gift shop and the Lyndhurst Tourist Information Centre.

MIDDLE WALLOP
Museum of Army Flying, Middle Wallop, near Stockbridge. Telephone: 0264 62121 extension 421/428.

Middle Wallop is the home of the Army Air Corps, formed in 1957, although the history of army flying goes back to the use of balloons and kites in the 1870s. The story includes the deeds of the Glider Pilot Regiment, which served with distinction during the liberation of Normandy in 1944, at the Arnhem landing and the crossing of the Rhine. The Horsa glider was capable of carrying 28 troops while the larger Hamilcar could carry a light tank into battle. As well as a glider, the displays include a remarkable experimental jeep fitted with rotor arms which, it was hoped, would allow it to be towed behind an aircraft into the battlefield.

The Army Air Corps now uses helicopters; among the earliest was the Skeeter, one of

HMS Alliance at the Royal Navy Submarine Museum, Gosport.

D-Day Museum, Portsmouth.

which is displayed in a collection of aircraft which includes a serviceable First World War Sopwith Pup and an Auster, developed for the Air Observation Post Squadrons in the Second World War.

PORTSMOUTH

Charles Dickens Birthplace Museum, 393 Commercial Road, Portsmouth. Telephone: 0705 827261. Portsmouth City Council.

Mile End is part of Landport well to the north of Old Portsmouth. Mile End Terrace, now called Commercial Road, was where Charles Dickens was born on 7th February 1812. Dickens's father was a clerk in the Navy Pay Office and it is said that the character of Mr Micawber was based upon him. The house in which Dickens was born is now opened as a small museum furnished as a middle-class family house of the early nineteenth century.

Cumberland House Museum, Eastern Parade, Southsea, Portsmouth PO4 9RF. Telephone: 0705 827261. Portsmouth City Council.

This is a museum of the natural history of the Portsmouth region and is the best natural history display in the region. Mole and Ratty from *Wind in the Willows* welcome the visitor with a lively display of a riverside habitat with live fish in an aquarium. The pace of the displays is maintained with a presentation of the geological profile of the Solent, followed by a gallery which is dominated by a reconstruction of a giant iguanodon. An audio-visual display tells the story of the solar system and the evolution of the earth.

Upstairs there are lively diorama reconstructions of the natural history of the chalk downland on Portsdown Hill and a reconstruction of a bird hide on Farlington Marshes.

Finally, the museum presents the visitors with the challenges of ecology in the modern urban world and concludes with an image of the most dangerous animal on earth: just press the button and a mirror is revealed!

D-Day Museum, Clarence Esplanade, Portsmouth. Telephone: 0705 827261. Portsmouth City Council.

The D-Day Museum, next to Southsea Castle, was built in 1984 to mark the fortieth anniversary of the D-Day landings in Normandy. It is the only museum in Britain which is devoted to the Normandy landings, and its centrepiece is the magnificent Overlord Embroidery. This modern counterpart to the Bayeux Tapestry was commissioned in 1968 by Lord Dulverton as a memorial and record of the Allied effort to liberate Europe during the Second World War. The 272 foot (83 metre) embroidery is made up of 34 panels which record the planning and the execution of Operation Overlord, the largest seaborne invasion in the history of man.

The D-Day Museum traces the history of Operation Overlord with a remarkable audio-visual presentation (in English, French and German). The museum also houses a large exhibition which retells the story of Portsmouth and its civilians during the war, the build-up to the great invasion and the battle of Normandy. Southwick House, to the north of

51

Portsmouth, was chosen as the headquarters for Operation Overlord and the original D-Day Operations Map is preserved there. A replica, with Montgomery and Eisenhower standing in front, is included in the museum.

Dockyard Apprentice Museum, Unicorn Training Centre, Unicorn Road, Portsmouth. Telephone: 0705 822571. Hampshire County Council.

The museum is housed in the training centre just outside the Naval Base's Unicorn Gate. It concentrates on the industrial aspects of ship-building and contains models and demonstration pieces made by the apprentices who trained in the dockyard. There is a fascinating collection of tools and a display of documents and old photographs of the dockyard.

Mary Rose, HM Naval Base, Portsmouth. Telephone: 0705 750521.

Henry VIII's flagship, the *Mary Rose,* is rightly one of the best known surviving warships in the world. The remains of the hull, raised from the muds of the Solent in 1982, are preserved in a dry dock close to HMS *Victory.* The dock has been covered so that the timbers can be kept moist by a continual spray of water, essential to the conservation of the hull. Here visitors can view the hull and the work of reconstructing the decks and other fittings removed during the archaeological excavations. About half the hull is now lost but the remains are displayed so that the visitor can view the interior as one would a dolls' house.

The excavation of the *Mary Rose,* which sank in 1545, has recovered a truly remarkable collection of objects, perfectly preserved in the Solent mud. This includes the great guns of the ship as well as personal belongings such as leather shoes and jerkins, and a unique collection of objects from the barber surgeon's cabin. The preservation of a vast range of everyday objects carried on board the ship makes the *Mary Rose* a perfectly preserved time capsule of life on a sixteenth-century warship. The objects, re-creations of scenes of life on board and displays illustrating Tudor social and maritime history are presented in the Mary Rose Exhibition housed in one of the dockyard's historic boathouses.

Portsmouth City Museum, Museum Road, Old Portsmouth PO1 2LJ. Telephone: 0705 827261. Portsmouth City Council.

The popular perception of Portsmouth is that it is predominantly a naval town but its history as a garrison town for the Army is equally important. The City Museum is appropriately housed in one of the few surviving Victorian army barracks, the Clarence Barracks, built in the 1880s, with a profusion of turrets and gables in the manner of a French *château.*

The museum houses an extensive collection of paintings, furniture and contemporary craft material. It is both an art gallery and a museum of local history for Portsmouth. There are displays on Victorian and later domestic life with good collections of toys and kitchen implements. There is a regular series of exhibitions including good art and craft exhibitions and local history displays.

Royal Marines Museum, Eastney Barracks, Eastney, Portsmouth. Telephone: 0705 819385.

This superb military museum is situated in the imposing former Officers' Mess, built in 1868, overlooking the parade ground of Eastney Barracks. Using audio-visual presentations, exciting models and dioramas, maps, photographs and paintings, the display traces the history of the amphibious regiment, the Royal Marines. There is a dramatic display on the First World War action at Zeebrugge and much on the Combined Operations which were vital to the success of the D-Day landing in 1944.

Amongst the many trophies on display is Napoleon's chair, from his period of exile on St Helena, and the Lewis gun used by Sergeant Finch, who won a Victoria Cross at Zeebrugge. The medal room includes the complete set of ten Victoria Crosses awarded to Royal Marines. There is an extensive display of uniforms, a room dedicated to the Royal Marines bands and an impressive display of regimental silver and pictures.

Royal Naval Museum, HM Naval Base, Portsmouth. Telephone: 0705 733060.

The Royal Naval Museum was opened in 1938 alongside HMS *Victory* and contains the Victory Collection displayed around the State Barge, which carried Nelson's body along the Thames during his funeral procession on 9th January 1806. The collection has been enriched by the addition of the McCarthy Collection of Nelson memorabilia, displayed in the eighteenth-century naval warehouse next to the museum. A visit to the museum, with its famous panorama of the battle of Trafalgar, must accompany a visit to HMS *Victory.*

The museum is not just a shrine to Horatio Nelson and HMS *Victory.* In recent years it has expanded into the adjacent row of eighteenth-century naval warehouses where displays tell the story of the development of the modern navy, its role in the two world wars and the South Atlantic campaign of 1982.

Southsea Castle Museum, Clarence Esplanade, Southsea, Portsmouth PO5 3PA. Telephone: 0705 827261. Portsmouth City Council.

The architecture and history of Henry VIII's castle at Southsea is dealt with in chapter 5.

The Portsmouth City Museum is housed in the former Clarence Barracks.

The keep contains displays on the fortifications of Portsmouth, which, in the eighteenth and nineteenth centuries, was the most fortified town in Europe. There are displays about the prisoners of war incarcerated in hulks in Portsmouth Harbour during the Napoleonic wars, including some fine ship models of the period.

HMS Victory, HM Naval Base, Portsmouth. Telephone: 0705 819604.

Portsmouth has the largest collection of naval heritage attractions in Britain, centred on the Naval Base with its unique collection of eighteenth- and nineteenth-century dockyard buildings. The most famous is Nelson's flagship at the battle of Trafalgar, HMS *Victory*. Built in Chatham in the 1760s, HMS *Victory* has been in continuous commission since 1778. The ship has been carefully restored and the visitor is able to look at the admiral's cabin, the captain's cabin, and the cramped accommodation on the gun decks where sailors slung their mess tables between the 32-pounder guns. The hellish roar of guns as the ship went into action can only be imagined, although the red paint of the orlop deck, which disguised the flow of blood in the sick bay, is a reminder of the gruesome realities of naval warfare almost two hundred years ago.

The visitor is taken to the cockpit where

Nelson died in a midshipman's berth at 4.30 in the afternoon of 21st October 1805 and where wreaths are placed every year on Trafalgar Day. Guided tours take the visitor to the quarter deck where there is a plaque marking the spot where Nelson fell, pierced by a musket ball through his left shoulder.

HMS Warrior, HM Naval Base, Portsmouth. Telephone: 0705 291379.

To complete the collection of Portsmouth's historic warships, Britain's first iron-hulled, armoured warship is berthed at a specially built jetty just inside the Naval Base. HMS *Warrior* was launched in 1860 as the world's largest, fastest and best protected warship. Her iron hull is armoured with wrought iron 4½ inches (114 mm) thick, backed by 18 inches (46 cm) of teak. She ended up as a floating jetty for fuelling ships at Milford Haven but over an eight-year period she has been fully restored to her former glory in a multi-million pound restoration scheme undertaken in Hartlepool.

SELBORNE

The Oates Memorial Library and Museum and Gilbert White Museum, The Wakes, Selborne, near Alton. Telephone: 042050 275.

The little village of Selborne is perhaps the last place in which one would expect to find a museum devoted to Captain Lawrence Oates,

53

The Wakes, Gilbert White's house in Selborne.

whose death on Scott's 1911 Antarctic Expedition epitomised the English ideal of an heroic gentleman. The Wakes was the house in which the famous eighteenth-century naturalist Gilbert White lived and its acquisition and conversion into a museum was made possible by R. W. Oates, who endowed a trust in memory of his family, hence its dual role as a museum. The Gilbert White collections are in the original part of the house, whilst those relating to the Oates family are in the nineteenth-century wing and on the first floor. There is also some local history, with displays on the archaeology of the nearby Selborne Priory.

The garden of The Wakes is being restored to its eighteenth-century form (see chaper 6). There are many local walks through the village 'hanger' or through the 'lythes', known to so many through the writings of Selborne's famous curate (see chapter 11).

SOUTHAMPTON

Bargate Museum, The Bargate, Southampton. Telephone: 0703 224216. Southampton City Council.

The medieval Bargate is one of the surviving gateways of the medieval town (see chapter 5). It is now a museum with exhibitions of local history. These have included the history of Southampton's trams and buses, local prints and photographs, the Southampton blitz and Southampton as a trooping port.

City Art Gallery, Commercial Road, Southampton. Telephone: Southampton 0703 832769. Southampton City Council.

Situated in the north block of the Civic Centre, the City Art Gallery is widely acclaimed as the finest in England south of London. It has extensive collections dating from the fourteenth-century to the present day. Although there are many outstanding works by European artists, including seventeenth-century Dutch paintings and French impressionists, the gallery is internationally renowned for its collection of twentieth-century British art, including many works by contemporary artists.

Hall of Aviation, Albert Road South, Southampton. Telephone: 0703 635830. Incorporates the R. J. Mitchell Memorial Museum.

This is a museum devoted to the long and fascinating story of aviation, mostly marine aviation, in and around the Solent. The legendary Supermarine Spitfire was designed and first built in Southampton and the museum displays a Mk 24 model as well as extensive material on the history of Supermarine. Also on display is one of the Supermarine racing seaplanes that took part in the Schneider Trophy events in the Solent in 1929 and 1931.

The centrepiece of the museum, and a feature around which it was designed, is a restored Sandringham flying boat with a wingspan of 114 feet (34 metres). Visitors can walk through the passenger cabins and gain some idea of the luxury of flying boat travel in the prewar days of the Empire routes.

Few people realise that Southampton was the birthplace of modern helicopter development and there are several on display including a 'Skeeter', one of the first helicopters used

54

by the British Army. Other aircraft include a Folland Gnat, the 1955 jet fighter, designed and built near Southampton, which became famous as the aircraft used by the Red Arrows.

Maritime Museum, Bugle Street, Southampton. Telephone: 0703 224216. Southampton City Council.

Housed in the early fifteenth-century Wool House (see chapter 6) the museum covers the extensive maritime history of Southampton, concentrating on the port since the growth of the docks in the nineteenth century. The exhibits on the ground floor include a 22 foot (7 metre) long model of the docks and a restored Itchen ferry boat (the local type of fishing boat, developed in the nineteenth century). There are displays on steamships, shipbuilding and local ferries, with several restored steam engines. The upper floor, devoted to the great liners, is dominated by a magnificent builder's model of the *Queen Mary*. There is a display on the *Titanic*, which sailed from Southampton on its ill-fated maiden voyage. There is also material on the story of speed at sea, based on the 1933 record-breaking speedboat, *Miss Britain III*, built at Hythe near Southampton.

Museum of Archaeology, God's House Tower, Town Quay, Southampton. Telephone: 0703 224216. Southampton City Council.

As with the other Southampton museums, the Museum of Archaeology is housed in a restored medieval building. Named after the adjacent medieval foundation of God's House, the tower was built in the early fifteenth century as the first purpose-built residential gun tower in Europe (see chapter 5).

The museum displays local prehistory (a collection of palaeolithic flints from local gravels) and the story of the three Southampton towns. The Romans had a small settlement at Bitterne on the river Itchen and, in the seventh century, the Saxon town of Hamwic was established near the present St Mary's part of the city. Archaeological work has shown this to have been the first planned town in post-Roman Europe and it is an archaeological site of international significance. More is known about the Saxon town of Hamwic than any other town of the late seventh and eighth centuries.

The medieval town, further to the west, on the shores of the river Test, was established in the tenth or eleventh century. Modern and imaginative displays in the museum tell the story of the medieval town, its merchants and its trade. These include pottery from the extensive collections which have made Southampton a centre for the study of medieval ceramics.

Tudor House Museum, St Michael's Square, Southampton. Telephone: 0703 224216. Southampton City Council.

The Tudor House is a late medieval timbered town house built by a rich Southampton merchant on the site of earlier houses, fragments of which can be discerned in the existing structure (see chapter 6). The building contains Southampton's museum of local and social history; there are extensive displays including Victorian room settings. There is also a comprehensive exhibition on middle-class life around 1900.

Perhaps the finest exhibit is the house itself: walking around the many rooms, staircases and corridors with their creaking floorboards gives the visitor a sense of the past.

A remarkable reconstruction of a Tudor Garden (opened in 1982) is one of the attractions at Tudor House (see chapter 6). At the rear of the Tudor Garden is the well preserved twelfth-century merchant's house, King John's House (see chapter 6).

WINCHESTER

Cathedral Treasury, Cathedral Office, 5 The Close, Winchester. Telephone: 0962 53137.

A collection of plate from the cathedral and from Hampshire parishes, the earliest dating from the fourteenth century, is displayed in a treasury at the west end of the cathedral. There is also a selection of the archaeological

The Hall of Aviation, Southampton.

finds discovered during the excavation of the Saxon Old Minster, precursor to the modern cathedral (see chapter 4).

City Museum, The Square, Winchester. Telephone: 0962 68166 extension 269. Winchester City Council.

The top floor has a fine collection of bronze age and iron age discoveries, including the important Owslebury burial. The room is dominated by a magnificent mosaic from the Roman villa at nearby Sparsholt. Extensive archaeological excavations have been carried out in Winchester since the 1950s, revealing a wealth of information about the Roman town of *Venta Belgarum* as well as the Saxon and medieval towns of Winchester. Winchester's archaeological collections rank amongst the best in the land but only the finest items are displayed on the ground floor of the museum.

The first floor of the museum is devoted to Winchester's local history, including the imaginatively displayed interior of a Victorian chemist's shop and the complete interior of a tobacconist's shop, both of which were rescued from the High Street.

Guildhall Picture Gallery, The Broadway, Winchester. Telephone: 0962 68166. Winchester City Council.

This is a small gallery with an interesting and varied programme of exhibitions by, mainly, local artists.

Royal Army Pay Corps Museum, Worthy Down, Winchester. Telephone: 0962 880880 extension 2435.

A small museum on an aspect of service history essential to the efficient functioning of an army, it was set up in 1977 and has an educational role within the Army Pay Corps as well as being open to the public.

Royal Green Jackets Museum, Peninsula Barracks, Winchester. Telephone: 0962 885522 extension 4216. Closed at present for reorganisation; expected to reopen 1989.

This is a museum worth a leisured visit. It houses the collections of the Royal Green Jackets and of the three regiments from which the present regiment was formed: the Oxfordshire and Buckinghamshire Light Infantry, the King's Royal Rifle Corps and the Rifle Brigade.

Amongst the fascinating array of trophies and memorabilia on display is the court dress worn by the first Duke of Wellington, the Iron Duke, when he was Colonel-in-Chief of the Rifle Brigade (founded in 1800 and amalgamated into the Royal Green Jackets in 1966).

There are relics of Sir John Moore, including the sashes used to lower his body into the grave at Corunna, immortalised in the lines:

'Not a drum was heard, not a funeral note, As his corpse to the rampart we hurried ...'
More recent history is recalled in a diorama commemorating the battle for the bridges over the Caen Canal on 6th June 1944.

Royal Hampshire Regiment Museum and Memorial Garden, Serle's House, Southgate Street, Winchester SO23 9EG. Telephone: 0962 63658.

Serle's House was built in about 1730 for one William Sheldon. In 1781 the house was sold to James Serle, an attorney, and it was James's son Peter who forged the link between the house and the military which has continued to the present day. Colonel Peter Serle commanded the South Hampshire Militia for the period 1804-26 and during his tenure of command used Serle's House for his headquarters. Shortly before his death in 1826 he sold the house to the government to ensure its continuance in this service.

Used briefly as judges' lodgings, the house again passed to the Hampshire Militia when, in 1881, the Hampshire Militia became the Third Battalion, The Hampshire Regiment, and, later, was instituted as headquarters of the regiment. The approach to the museum is through a very beautiful Memorial Garden opened in 1952, to the memory of men of the regiment who have fallen in battle.

Royal Hussars Museum, Southgate Street, Winchester SO23 9EF. Telephone: 0962 63751.

The Royal Hussars (Prince of Wales's Own) were formed in 1969 by the amalgamation of two cavalry regiments, both of which were raised in 1715: the 10th Royal Hussars (Prince of Wales's Own) and the 11th Hussars (Prince Albert's Own). Both regiments had distinguished records, covering all the campaigns in Europe, Asia Minor, the Crimea, Egypt, South Africa and India. Both were involved in the battle of El Alamein.

The colourful and imaginative display in the museum tells the history of both regiments through the media of pictures, photographs, medals, uniforms, weapons and silver.

Westgate Museum, High Street, Winchester. Telephone: 0962 68166 extension 269. Winchester City Museum.

The Westgate controlled access to the medieval town on the road to Romsey and there is evidence that there was a gateway here during the Saxon period. The building has been described (see chapter 5); inside there is a fine little museum. The main feature is a sixteenth-century painted wooden ceiling, originally from Winchester College, which may have been designed and built to celebrate the anticipated visit to Winchester College by

Mary I when she was married to Philip II of Spain in Winchester in 1554.

Winchester Gallery, Winchester School of Art, Park Avenue, Winchester. Telephone: 0962 842500.

This gallery specialises in the display of modern art and craft. There is a regular programme of exhibitions that do for Winchester and its area what the Southampton City Art Gallery does for Southampton and the region. The exhibits are of very fine quality and the gallery is well worth a visit.

Winchester Heritage Centre, 52-4 Upper Brook Street, Winchester. Telephone: 0962 51664.

This is a heritage centre in the traditional mould, with exhibitions on the architecture of the city and contemporary planning and conservation issues. There is a permanent exhibition and an audio-visual display on the historical development of Winchester which complement the displays in the City Museum.

Lymington Harbour.

The Hawk Conservancy, Weyhill, near Andover.

9
Other places to visit

Birdworld Park and Gardens, Holt Pound, Bentley. Telephone: 0420 22140.

On the border of Hampshire and Surrey, between Basingstoke and Farnham, the gardens, woodland and parks contain a huge variety of birds including vultures, flamingos, pelicans and parrots. At Penguin Island the birds can be seen swimming behind large sheets of glass. Visitors can either walk around the park or travel on the safari ride.

Birdworld is also home of 'Underwater World' which houses a fascinating collection of fish from the lakes, rivers and seas of the world.

Denmead Pottery Limited, Denmead, near Waterlooville. Telephone: 0705 261942.

The village of Denmead is the home of one of the few large commercial potteries outside Stoke-on-Trent. At specific times on weekdays visitors can tour the factory to see all aspects of the production process.

The pottery is located in 20 acres (8 ha) of landscaped grounds with a lake, woodland walks and picnic areas, together with an adventure playground for children. The factory shop sells production-line seconds, ranging from lampbases to casseroles.

Finkley Down Farm and Country Park. On the A303, 2 miles (3 km) east of Andover. Telephone: 0264 52195.

Finkley Down Farm has a comprehensive selection of rare and not so rare breeds of farm animals and poultry, rearing their young in a natural environment rarely seen in these days of commercialisation. There are ponies, Shire horses, cattle, sheep, pigs, goats and poultry. There is also a pets' corner where children can handle the rabbits, lambs, kids and other animals.

Hawk Conservancy, Weyhill, near Andover. Telephone: 026477 2252. Just off the A303 4 miles (6 km) west of Andover.

The Hawk Conservancy has the largest collection of birds of prey in southern England. Visitors can see and photograph hawks, falcons, owls, vultures and kites from all over the world. Birds are trained using traditional methods and there are daily demonstrations of the birds in flight.

The centre carries out breeding of many species and there is a comprehensive educational programme, including lectures and demonstrations of flying.

Longdown Dairy Farm, Deerleap Lane, Longdown, Ashurst, near Southampton. Telephone: 042129 3326.

This is a working farm which welcomes visitors to come and see 'behind the scenes'. Here the visitor can watch the daily milking of the herd of 150 pedigree Friesians, each of which produces 1200 gallons (5500 litres) of milk each year.

According to the season children and adults can watch orphan lambs being reared and chicks hatching in an incubator or can stroke a newborn calf.

Marwell Zoological Park, Colden Common, near Winchester. Telephone: 096274 406.

Set in over 100 acres (40 ha) of Hampshire countryside, Marwell is one of the largest zoos in Britain and one of the most famous. It was established in the 1970s to establish a breeding centre for endangered species, still an important part of Marwell's work. The zoo has a fine collection of hoofed animals and some of the herds are now providing animals for reintroduction into the wild in their native countries. Marwell specialises in big cats including Asian lions, Siberian tigers, snow leopards, jaguars, cheetahs and many others. There are also all the zoo favourites such as giraffes, monkeys, rhinoceroses, zebras and camels.

New Forest Butterfly Farm, Longdown, Ashurst, near Southampton. Telephone: 042129 2166.

The New Forest Butterfly Farm is a living display of native and exotic butterflies and moths. The principal feature is an indoor tropical jungle crowded with colourful butterflies from South America, Malaysia and beyond. The butterflies, some of which have wing spans of 10 inches (25 cm), fly freely amongst the visitors. The life cycle of the butterfly can be studied in detail: females can be seen laying eggs and, on the leaves, caterpillars and pupae can be seen before they emerge as the imago, or young adult.

An extension to the main, solar-heated building is devoted to the British butterfly and here there are garden plants, nettles, brambles and grasses which are so important to the preservation of native butterflies both in town and country.

Outside there are dragonfly ponds. The New Forest is an outstanding area for dragonflies and damselflies, so there is a good chance that on most days in the season a number of species will be seen breeding in and around the ponds.

Paultons Park, Ower, near Romsey SO51 6AL. Telephone: 0703 814442.

Set in 140 acres (57 ha) of parkland which originally surrounded a magnificent country

A Reading wagon in the Romany Museum, Paultons Park, Ower.

CHAPTER 9

house, now demolished, and well situated for visitors to the New Forest area, Paultons Park is one of the county's biggest tourist attractions.

There is a wide variety of individual features ranging from 'Capt'n Blood's Cavern' to a flora and fauna board walk. Paultons Park is well known for its large collection of exotic birds and animals and has well established gardens, ranged round a lake.

There is an extensive collection of Romany caravans, housed in a Romany Museum. The way of life around 1900 is depicted in the Village Life Museum.

There are many attractions for children including a large adventure playground. A Rio Grande train takes visitors round the park.

Portsmouth Sea Life Centre, Clarence Esplanade, Southsea, Portsmouth. Telephone: 0705 734461.

The great attraction of the Sea Life Centre is the chance to view the great variety of fish and other animals that are normally only seen by divers. Specially constructed giant sheets of glass enable the visitor to look for cod, crab, lobsters and a host of other creatures as they weave between anchors and sunken ships. The centre also includes a replica ship's bridge and an audio-visual theatre.

Viables Craft Centre, Harrow Way, Basingstoke. Telephone: 0256 473634.

This craft community, working in converted farm buildings, welcomes visitors, who can examine the craft workshops, including those of goldsmiths and silversmiths, potters, glass engravers, makers of reproduction antique dolls and soft toys, metal engravers, spinners and weavers, and many more. The craft centre supplies high-quality goods and undertakes commissioned works.

Wellington Country Park, Riseley, near Reading. Telephone: 0734 326444. On the B3349 between Reading and Alton.

The Wellington Country Park was opened in 1974, having been landscaped around a flooded gravel pit, now an attractive 40 acre (16 ha) lake well stocked with coarse fish. The lake is used for a wide range of individual and family activities including angling, sunbathing or watching the wildfowl (on the banks) and canoeing, windsurfing and boating (on the water).

There are five waymarked nature trails through the surrounding woods, one of which passes through a deer park containing both red and fallow deer. As with most centres of this type there are numerous activities for children, including an adventure playground, crazy golf and a miniature steam railway.

In 1978 the Prince of Wales opened the National Dairy Museum which illustrates the development of the dairy industry since the days of Waterloo. An addition to the park which is of particular interest to young children is the Thames Valley Time Trail.

10
Tourist information centres

Aldershot: Military Museum, Queen's Avenue, Aldershot GU11 2LG. Telephone: 0252 20968.
Andover: Town Mill Car Park, Bridge Street, Andover. Telephone: 0264 24320.
Beaulieu: John Montagu Building, Beaulieu SO42 7ZN. Telephone: 0590 713196.
Eastleigh: Town Hall Centre, Leigh Road, Eastleigh SO5 4DE. Telephone: 0703 274741/21333 extension 1184.
Fareham: Ferneham Hall, Osborn Road, Fareham PO16 7DB. Telephone: 0329 221342.
Farnborough: Divisional Library, Pinehurst Avenue, Farnborough GU14 1JZ. Telephone: 0252 513838 extension 24.
Gosport: Falkland Gardens, Gosport PO12 1EJ. Telephone: 0705 522944.
Havant: 1 Park Road South, Havant PO9 1HA. Telephone: 0705 480024.
Lyndhurst: Main Car Park, Lyndhurst. Telephone: 042128 2269.
Petersfield: The Library, 27 The Square, Petersfield GU32 3HH.
Portsmouth: The Hard, Portsmouth PO1 3QJ. Telephone: 0705 826722.
Ringwood: Furlong Lane Car Park, Ringwood BH24 1AZ. Telephone: 0425 470896.
Romsey: Bus Station Car Park, Broadwater Road, Romsey SO5 8GT.
Rownhams Service Area, M27 (westbound). Telephone: 0703 730345.
Southampton: Above Bar Shopping Precinct, Above Bar Street, Southampton SO9 4XF. Telephone: 0703 221106.
Southsea: Clarence Esplanade, Southsea PO5 3PE. Telephone: 0705 754358.
Southsea Continental Ferryport, Albert Johnson Quay, Mile End, Southsea. Telephone: 0705 698111.
Winchester: The Guildhall, The Broadway, Winchester SO23 9JZ. Telephone: 0962 65406.

11
Towns and villages

ALDERSHOT

Aldershot and its neighbour, Farnborough, were formed into the district of Rushmoor in 1974. When the military first came to the area in 1855 the two towns were then small villages. Both grew as the civilian population expanded to meet the needs of the growing military town: Aldershot to serve the South Camp and the army; Farnborough to serve the North Camp. The latter became famous for its association with aviation.

The military town of Aldershot impresses the visitor with its stark monotony of military buildings and acres of married quarters, although many improvements have been made in recent decades. However, it is well worth visiting for its regimental museums and heritage centre (see chapter 8).

All Saints' church is the garrison church of the British Army. It contains memorials that bring to mind wars in many parts of the world since Victorian times. Near the church is the giant Wellington Memorial, an equestrian statue designed by Matthew Wyatt for Constitution Arch in London. It was later thought to be too large for the arch and was moved to its present site in 1883.

The Rushmoor Arena, home of the almost legendary prewar Aldershot Tattoo, has recently been restored to its former splendour and is worth a visit.

ALRESFORD

There is Old Alresford and New Alresford, which was laid out as a planned town by the Bishop of Winchester about 1200. The church in Old Alresford is worth a visit as it is a fine eighteenth-century building and contains a memorial which records the fact that Mary Sumner founded the Mothers' Union in Old Alresford in 1875. Alresford House is now open to the public (see chapter 6).

New Alresford can hardly fail to charm, with Broad Street, broad as its name implies, stretching from the church to Old Alresford Pond. It has been described as Hampshire's best village street. Throughout the middle ages wool and cloth created wealth for the town while the pond provided power for the fulling mills. New Alresford was burnt down in 1689 with the result that many of the houses date from the seventeenth and eighteenth centuries.

ALTON

Alton was formerly well known for its smells, as brewing has been the major industry here for at least two centuries. It is now an old country market town with a charming, curved high street and a small market square. In earlier times the town had the advantage of much trade from its position on the London to Winchester road, although the 'Pass of Alton' was notorious in the thirteenth century for its robbers.

At the top of Amery Street there is the house where the Elizabethan poet Edmund Spenser spent his latter years, before his death in 1599. William Curtis, the famous eighteenth-century botanist, was born in a fine house in Lenten Street. The present Curtis Museum was opened by a nineteenth-century successor of this famous native of Alton (see chapter 8).

One gruesome story involves the association of Alton with the origin of the aphorism 'Sweet Fanny Adams'. This was the name of an eight-year-old girl murdered in a nearby hop field in August 1867. The subsequent trial of the murderer and the extensive coverage of the macabre details in the press coincided with the introduction of a much disliked tinned mutton in the Royal Navy. The sailors likened the contents of the tins to the remains of the murdered girl and in due course 'Sweet F A' came to mean 'nothing of substance at all'!

St Lawrence's church is worth a visit. It was the scene of a heroic battle in December 1643 when the Royalist Captain John Bolle took refuge with his men and refused to surrender. He was slain as he fought in the pulpit and the damage caused by gun shot can still be seen in the church door.

ANDOVER

Andover has a history dating back to Saxon times. The town was burnt down in 1434 but there are few surviving buildings that date to the subsequent reconstruction. Later, the town's importance was both as a local market centre and a staging post on the road from London to the south-west. During the 1960s the town's population was increased from 16,000 to almost 50,000 as part of the London overspill programme. Large housing estates have been built with ring roads that avoid the old town centre.

The wide southern part of the High Street has the excellent classical town hall of 1825, and near this is the Danebury (formerly the Star and Garter) Hotel of about the same date. Many of the original frontages survive along the High Street, which climaxes in the church of St Mary situated on a slight hill. The church was built in the early 1840s and has an impressive interior crowned with make-believe plaster vaulting (see chapter 4). Near the church is the Andover Museum which houses the Museum of the Iron Age (see chapter 8).

BASINGSTOKE

In 1961 Basingstoke was chosen to be the home of some 60,000 Londoners who were to come to this small market town as part of a huge expansion scheme. Since then the rich agricultural hinterland has been covered with housing estates together with warehouses, factories and offices, which came to the new town with its excellent communications.

The modernity of the town centre has an interest of its own and there are a few interesting buildings of earlier periods, including the seventeenth-century Queen Anne House in Church Street and the Town Hall of 1832 in High Street. The church of St Michael is over-restored Perpendicular with a fine two-storey south porch. For a town such as Basingstoke the museum is of quite exceptional quality (see chapter 8).

The romantic ruins of the medieval Holy Ghost chapel stand on Chapel Hill with the fragments of the Guild Chapel built by Lord Sandys of The Vyne (see chapter 6) in 1524. The cemetery there is said to date from the papal interdict during the reign of King John, which forbade burials in churchyards.

BEAULIEU

For most visitors Beaulieu is just the Motor Museum and Palace House, but the village is one of great interest. Until fifty years ago local sailing craft, the Cowes ketches which carried bulk cargoes such as corn between Southampton, Poole, Portsmouth and the Isle of Wight, would sail up the Beaulieu River to the village at its head. The lake is tidal and one of the houses on the causeway that encloses the lake contains a mill driven by the flow of the tide as at Eling (see chapter 7). The Montagu Arms dates from 1888.

BISHOP'S WALTHAM

The regular pattern of the streets in Bishop's Waltham suggests that it was one of the planned towns established by the Bishops of Winchester in the thirteenth century, and that there was originally a large market square, now built over by subsequent encroachments. There was also a town here before the middle ages as the church enjoyed the status of an important minster during the Saxon period.

Bishop's Waltham is a pleasant town, overlooked by the church on the high ground. The best way to approach it is from the north: the road dips down into the narrow sloping streets. At the centre is George Square from which the broad High Street runs. The town is better known for its atmosphere of a somewhat forgotten market town than for any buildings of particular architectural merit. One interest-

ing association is the fact that Bank Street was the home of Gunner's Bank, the last private bank in Britain.

The remains of the Bishops' Palace at Bishop's Waltham are rightly famous and should be visited (see chapter 6).

BROCKENHURST

Brockenhurst is in essence a New Forest village. The church of St Peter claims to be the oldest in the Forest. This may be the case but the additions of later ages, such as the brick tower of 1761, give it a character of its own. The churchyard is famous for its gravestones. Here the tombs of a hundred New Zealanders who died at a nearby hospital during the First World War are a reminder of how global conflict can touch even this remote and peaceful spot. There is also a gravestone bearing the carving of a little hut. It commemorates a famous forest character, Brusher Mills, who lived in his hut for thirty years, making his living by catching live adders.

Nearby is the remarkable Rhinefield Lodge, built in 1888-90 for Lionel Walker Munroe by Romaine-Walker. It is large, with extravagant Tudor and Gothic features, including a massive banqueting hall with a hammerbeam roof. One of the features of the house is the Alhambra smoking room built as a re-creation of the Spanish palace. The gardens at Rhinefield are now being restored to their original late nineteenth-century design.

One of the great features of the New Forest is the Rhinefield Ornamental Drive. It was laid out in the middle of the nineteenth century along a track that led to the predecessor of Rhinefield Lodge. Some of the trees are now of enormous height. For instance, there is a redwood of 137 feet (42 metres) and Douglas firs of over 150 feet (46 metres). There is a signposted trail called the Tall Trees Walk which has been laid out by the Forestry Commission.

BUCKLER'S HARD

Nowhere else is there a village which still has such a pervasive sense of the past. There is only one street, a broad space between two rows of brick cottages which reach up from the bank of the Beaulieu River. The whole village is a museum and has been treated as such by the Beaulieu estate, which operates it as one of Hampshire's main tourist attractions (see chapter 8).

Walking down the village street towards the hard on which so many of the wooden warships of Nelson's era were built, one can visit the small chapel or, further down, the Master Builder's House, now a hotel and public house. There are extensive walks along the banks of the Beaulieu River, past Bailey's Hard to Beaulieu village.

Union Street, Fareham.

BURSLEDON

In the late eighteenth century a bridge was built across the river Hamble at Bursledon as part of the route connecting Southampton, via the Northam Bridge, to Portsmouth. Here the river broadens out into a wide sweep encircled by low, wood-covered hills, a picturesque setting for the boat yards and marina berths which now crowd the water. The best place to admire the river setting is the Jolly Sailor public house.

Just next to the Jolly Sailor is the Elephant Yard, named after the ship launched at that spot and which carried Nelson into the battle of Copenhagen. The area was famous for shipbuilding during the Napoleonic wars and in the church there is a monument to Philemon Ewer, who died in 1750 and who 'during the late war with France and Spain built seven large ships of war'.

EASTLEIGH

The town owes its existence to the decision of the London and South Western Railway in 1891 to build their workshops and carriage works on the flat lands of the lower Itchen valley north of Southampton. In January 1895 the Urban District of Eastleigh was formed. It is now a large district covering neighbouring Chandler's Ford and North Stoneham, both dormitory suburbs to Southampton.

The railway works are now much in decline but the town has plenty of interesting public buildings, such as the railway station designed by William Tite in the 1840s. The best

(although damaged by fire) is the Church of the Resurrection, built by Street in 1868. Later additions include a south aisle by Sir Arthur Blomfield. The museum (see chapter 8) in the High Street is in the Citadel Hall.

ELING

The visitor is likely to come to Eling in search of the tide mill (see chapter 7) at the head of a little creek near the very top of Southampton Water. For centuries it was a lively port serving the New Forest hinterland and markets as far away as Salisbury. Coastal shipping was once very important around the New Forest shore and Eling retains its quay which still sees the occasional cargo ship. The port has expanded to the north to form the modern Totton, an important suburb to the west of Southampton.

On the top of the hill overlooking the little creek is the church of St Mary, which, although heavily restored in 1863, has many medieval and even some Saxon features. There is an interesting Italian, sixteenth-century Last Supper which may have been given by Lord Sandys of The Vyne (see chapter 6), who was a patron of the church. There are many associations with Eling, not least being the entry in the register recording a marriage conducted by Lord Protector Richard Cromwell.

FAREHAM

Pevsner has described Fareham High Street as one of the best country-town streets in the

63

South of England. Without stopping to explore the town the visitor can pass through with the impression that it is just part of the suburban sprawl between Portsmouth and Southampton.

Fareham was probably established as a market centre by the Bishops of Winchester in the thirteenth century. It was in Georgian times that it flourished most, as naval officers preferred to live here rather than in Portsmouth itself. The High Street has survived largely unaltered, having impressive lines of eighteenth-century houses, with elegant porches and doorcases, on either side. On the west side of the street is the parish church of St Peter and St Paul (see chapter 4) set in a large churchyard.

FARNBOROUGH

The world associates Farnborough with aviation: the regular Air Show brings tens of thousands of visitors to the Royal Aircraft Establishment. Farnborough was once a village but it grew with the military and now merges with the neighbouring military town of Aldershot.

What an unlikely place for the end of the Napoleonic dynasty! Napoleon III and the Empress Eugénie fled to England in 1870 after the disastrous Franco-Prussian war. Three years later the Emperor died and his widow moved to Farnborough where she acquired Farnborough Hill. In 1887 she built a vast mausoleum. In a vaulted crypt there are three large and impressive granite sarcophagi, each weighing over 5 tons. The Emperor lies in one. In another lies the Prince Imperial, who died fighting with British troops in the Zulu wars. In the third lies the Empress Eugénie herself, who died in 1920, aged 94. It is a remarkable monument to the dynasty and the politics which governed the fate of Europe for much of the nineteenth century. The Empress also established St Michael's Abbey, built in 1886 and partly modelled on Solesmes in France. It is now an abbey dependent on the Abbey of Prinknash near Gloucester.

FLEET

Fleet is a large, sprawling residential town, in the north of the county, near Farnborough and Aldershot. The church of All Saints, built 1861-2, is by William Burges. Fleet Pond is the biggest in Hampshire, covering some 130 acres (53 ha). The London to Southampton railway line cuts the pond in two, so the best views are to be had from the train!

FORDINGBRIDGE

The main feature of this small market town to the north of the New Forest is the fifteenth-century bridge with its seven pointed arches over the river Avon. The bridge was widened in the eighteenth century. Fordingbridge is a noted centre for fishermen: the local coarse fishing is famous for its pike. The town was once the centre of an important calico printing industry.

Although Fordingbridge is a charming little town, there are few buildings of note. The Gothic town hall of 1877 was originally the Oddfellows Hall, and adjacent to this is a row of shops, an architectural gem, dating from the late seventeenth or early eighteenth century.

By the river there is a statue of Augustus John by Ivor Robert-Jones. John lived at the nearby Fryern Court.

GOSPORT

This is a town that entirely owes its existence to the naval and military presence at Portsmouth, to which it was linked by a floating bridge as early as 1837. In 1855 a local guide book made the comment that Gosport occupied a small peninsula, 'and has risen to importance as a convenient appendage to Portsmouth'.

The eighteenth- and nineteenth-century fortifications of Gosport are dealt with elsewhere (see chapter 5). An excellent place for the visitor is the mid nineteenth-century Fort Brockhurst in which there is a notable exhibition on the development of fortifications around Gosport and Portsmouth.

Perhaps the most famous Naval establishment is the Haslar Royal Naval Hospital which was built in 1746-61, when it was the largest hospital in Europe and the biggest brick building in England. Clarence Yard was the main victualling yard for the Navy while Priddy's Hard was, and still is, a major ordnance depot. There is a magnificent small museum of naval ordnance here (chapter 8). Gosport also has a fine local history museum in Walpole Road (see chapter 8). In 1905 HMS *Dolphin* was established at Fort Blockhouse as the navy's first submarine base. It still serves this important function and houses the very fine Submarine Museum (see chapter 8).

Much of Gosport was flattened during the bombing of the Second World War and there are few buildings of note. The finest is Holy Trinity Church with its outstanding classical colonnades (see chapter 4), while the dramatic ruin of Gosport Railway Station of 1842, with its long range of Tuscan columns, is not to be missed.

HAMBLE

Hamble River is one of Britain's leading yachting havens. The little village of Hamble, with its curving main street of Georgian houses, is as picturesque as any Cornish fishing village. Hamble's history is the history of the sea: the village saw the great flagship of Henry V's navy, the *Grace Dieu,* laid up in the river before it was burnt to the waterline after being struck by lightning. The remains of the hull can still be seen at very low tides in the muds just above the Bursledon Bridge. Ships for Nelson's navy were built at several sites on the lower reaches of the Hamble and, later, there was an important oyster fishing fleet based at the village. The Solent was the cradle of marine aviation and the churchyard at Hamble contains the grave of the great aviation pioneer, Alliot Vernon Roe, whose company, Avro, established a factory near Hamble during the First World War.

HAMBLEDON

Broadhalfpenny Down, a mile or so north-east of Hambledon, is venerated the world over as the birthplace of cricket. The Hambledon Cricket Club came into existence about 1750 and in 1777 the club won against an All England team. All this is commemorated on a granite memorial near the Bat and Ball Inn at Broadhalfpenny Down.

Hambledon village has a long main street straggling along the floor of the valley between the chalklands and the coastal plain of Hampshire. Apart from the church, an interesting survival from earlier times is Manor Farm, which incorporates a thirteenth-century stone house. A fire in the eighteenth century destroyed part of the village, which now contains a fine selection of Georgian houses built of brick.

The now substantial English wine industry has its origins in the founding of the Hambledon Vineyard by Major-General Sir Guy Salisbury-Jones in the 1950s. The vines are on the south slope of Windmill Hill and produce some of the finest wines in Britain.

HARTLEY WINTNEY

Right up in the north of the county, Hartley Wintney owes its existence to the building of the turnpike, now the A30, in 1767. The village sprawls along the main road which, until the construction of the M3, was crowded with heavy traffic. Nowadays the visitor arriving from London is likely to miss this charming village unless a special effort is made to turn off the motorway and to seek out the pleasing elegance of the eighteenth-century houses and coaching inns, one of which, the White Lion, is said to have housed King George III en route to the sea bathing at Weymouth.

HAVANT

Ralph Dutton's famous book on Hampshire made only one remark on Havant: 'a town where one need not delay'. Havant, overlooking Langstone Harbour, is one of Hampshire's fast-growing towns, but it has had an interesting history, reflected in the church, which has structures of many periods. The museum, with its display of the famous Vokes Collection of firearms, is well worth a visit (see chapter 8). One of the main attractions of Havant is Leigh Park, laid out in the picturesque tradition in the early nineteenth century (see chapter 6).

HURSLEY

The history of Hursley Park, to the west of Winchester, is long and fascinating. On the north side of the park are the earthwork remains of Merdon Castle, a Norman castle whose ramparts still rise 50 feet (15 metres) above the moat. The house was first built in the fifteenth century and for a time it was the home of Richard Cromwell. During the eighteenth and nineteenth centuries it was the seat of the Heathcotes, one of the great Hampshire families of the Victorian era. In 1902 the house was bought by G. A. Cooper (of marmalade fame), who altered the building substantially, so making it into one of the great country houses of Edwardian England. In 1940 it was requisitioned by the Ministry of Aircraft Production for the relocation of Supermarine Aviation, whose works in Southampton had been destroyed by bombing. Now Hursley Park is the home of IBM.

The church of All Saints is of great importance in the history of the Church of England (see chapter 4). It was built in 1846-8 for John Keble, leader of the Oxford Movement, who paid for it from the royalties of his *The Christian Year*.

The village of Hursley is a delightful assemblage of houses, displaying a variety of vernacular styles which reflect the history of the village over many centuries.

LYMINGTON

Market day Saturday.

Lymington is the main market town and port of the New Forest. The borough was founded in the twelfth century, along with Yarmouth on the Isle of Wight, to provide a link with the Island. The harbour was within the Port of Southampton during the middle ages, and flourishing trades based on the import of wine and the export of cloth developed.

During the eighteenth century Lymington acquired popularity as a place for retirement and it was during this period that the long, elegant High Street acquired its present appearance. The church of St Thomas, with its seventeenth-century tower and eighteenth-century cupola, provides it with a visual climax.

In the 1830s a steamboat ferry service was established to link the port with the Isle of Wight, and, still, thousands of visitors pass through on their way to the island, barely pausing to enjoy the pleasures of the town.

The pretty harbour is now a major centre for yachting on the Solent.

Market day at Lymington is well worth a visit. The rows of stalls in the High Street are much as they have been for generations.

LYNDHURST

Both in the geographical and the administrative sense, Lyndhurst is the heart of the New Forest. The ancient Verderers' Court, which governs the Forest, meets at the Verderers' Hall at Lyndhurst. The Tourist Information Centre at Lyndhurst car park is a good place from which to plan a visit to the New Forest.

When the Lyndhurst bypass is built, then the main street will be worth a visit. One of the present attractions of Lyndhurst is the butcher's shop which specialises in the sale of venison.

St Michael's church is one of the finest Victorian churches in Hampshire (see chapter 4).

MINSTEAD

Minstead is one of the many villages of the New Forest. There is a small green with a shop, and a public house whose signboard (the original of which is in Winchester College) bears the image of the Trusty Servant. Just up the lane there is the charming church, which has changed little since the eighteenth century (see chapter 4). Sitting outside the hostelry on a warm summer day, while the ponies graze nearby, is one of the delights of the New Forest.

NORTH WARNBOROUGH

The exploration of the Basingstoke Canal (see chapter 7) will bring the visitor to North Warnborough. It has a charming little group of cottages and houses, including a fifteenth-century thatched cottage of cruck construction.

Nearby there is Odiham Castle, of which all that remains is the picturesque ruin of the keep built in 1207-12. It is unusual in being the only octagonal keep in England. Odiham has the distinction of being a royal castle and King John came here after he had been forced to sign the Magna Carta at Runnymede.

ODIHAM

Odiham is one of the most attractive of the small towns in Hampshire. The town is almost unique in the county in that the medieval street plan appears to have remained unchanged for three or four hundred years. Its main feature is a long, winding main street on either side of which are mellow brick frontages, decorated with bow windows and classical doorcases, with hardly anything distracting from the pleasing effect. To the south of

the High Street is the church, large, but not outstanding, although the seventeenth-century brick tower does complement the houses below.

There are several interesting curiosities at the church including a hudd (a sentry-box-like shelter to protect the parson at funerals when it was raining) and an interesting series of brasses. Near the churchyard wall are the old stocks and whipping post.

One of the most interesting buildings is The Priory, which is of three ranges. Although it has an eighteenth-century frontage, the main structure is Tudor.

PETERSFIELD

Petersfield was founded as a new borough by the Earl of Gloucester in the middle of the twelfth century. At the centre of the street plan is the large square market place which is now dominated by an equestrian statue of William III: a Dutch king on an English throne and here dressed as a Roman emperor. To the south of the market place is the church with its splendid Norman interior (see chapter 4).

A market town, Petersfield grew rich on wool and cloth but declined in the seventeenth century. As with many of the smaller towns of Hampshire, its appearance today owes much to the restoration of its fortunes in the eighteenth century, when it was an important staging post on the London to Portsmouth road.

There are many interesting buildings in the streets of Petersfield: the Red Lion (an old coaching inn), the Old College of 1729, and many houses and shops, with either brick fronts or flint nogging in timber frames. Sheep Street connects The Square with another open space now known as The Spain. This was originally a second market square, but now, grassed over, it looks like a village green.

PORTCHESTER

The Roman fort dominates this little village at the head of Portsmouth Harbour: spectacular views are to be had from the top of the keep (see chapters 3 and 5). Inside the castle is the church (see chapter 4), one of the finest in Hampshire, but the original settlement is now entirely swallowed up in the urban sprawl which stretches from Portsmouth to Fareham. There is a little huddle of, mostly, eighteenth-century houses in the lee of the castle. Together they form a delightful village setting, wholly unexpected during the drive from the A27 through rows of modern houses.

PORTSMOUTH

Only a short introduction to Portsmouth is needed here as the main visitor attractions have been covered elsewhere (see chapters 4, 5 and 8). Portsmouth covers an island, Portsea

Island, on the east of which is Langstone Harbour and on the west Portsmouth Harbour. Access to the island used to be via a gap in the defensive lines at Hilsea and, even now, with a motorway running almost to the heart of the city, leaving the island on a Friday evening can take a long time.

Portsmouth has played a strategic role in the defence of the realm for over 450 years. From the town defences of Henry VII to the giant forts of the nineteenth century, Portsmouth has the most comprehensive collection of fortifications in western Europe (see chapter 5). HMS *Victory*, HMS *Warrior*, the Royal Naval Museum and the *Mary Rose*, all based in the historic dockyard, now form the premier naval heritage collection in Britain (see chapter 8).

Portsmouth has much to offer apart from its naval and military heritage. Old Portsmouth, with its long High Street, much rebuilt after the war, has many buildings of note. The cathedral, with its curious mixture of styles, is well worth a visit (see chapter 4). There is the house in which the Duke of Buckingham was murdered, on 3rd August 1628, and further down the street is Grand Parade, with its views of the Garrison Church (see chapter 4). From the bottom of High Street one can walk to the little huddle of buildings and streets at The Point, which overlooks the entrance to Portsmouth Harbour. There is the feeling that it has changed little since Nelson's time. The Camber is the charming little harbour around which Old Portsmouth developed and here one can enjoy a quiet drink overlooking the fishing boats and the Isle of Wight ferries. After many decades of decline, wartime destruction and dereliction, Old Portsmouth is again flourishing and fashionable.

Portsea is the area between Old Portsmouth and the Dockyard. By the late eighteenth century this too had been enclosed within the town defences. Here there is the Common Hard, with Portsmouth Harbour railway station. A major feature of the Hard is HMS *Warrior*, now moored at a specially built jetty (see chapter 8).

Landport is the commercial and municipal centre of Portsmouth. Here there is the main railway station and the Guildhall, opened in 1890. The postwar reconstruction of the Guildhall and Guildhall Square is an impressive piece of urban design.

Southsea is on the south side of Portsea Island. It developed as a fashionable residential suburb during the nineteenth century and retains much of this character today. Southsea Common separates the town from the seaside proper with Clarence Pier and South Parade Pier. The Common is not only ideal for a walk in the bracing sea air: there are tennis courts, skating rinks and rock gardens. Further east,

past Southsea Castle (see chapter 5) one comes to the extensive Canoe Lake near the Lumps Fort. Southsea Esplanade then continues to Eastney, on the west of Portsea Island, where there is the Royal Marines museum (see chapter 8) and the historic Eastney Pumping Station (see chapter 7).

RINGWOOD

Overlooking the valley of the river Avon, Ringwood has always been an important crossing to the west. Much of the medieval town layout, based on the market square opposite the church, survives today. One of the buildings in High Street is interesting in that it was the house in which the Duke of Monmouth sheltered after the battle of Sedgemoor, prior to his removal and swift execution in London.

Another victim of the Monmouth Rebellion was Dame Alice Lisle, who lived at the nearby Moyles Court and is buried in the churchyard at Ellingham, not far from Ringwood. She was sentenced to death by burning by the notorious Judge Jeffries, but the sentence was commuted to decapitation and Dame Alice died in The Square at Winchester on 2nd September 1685.

Ringwood is the home of the Armfield Foundry which provided hydro-turbines for watermills all over Britain during the nineteenth and early twentieth centuries.

ROMSEY
Market day Friday.

Romsey is the small market town of Hampshire *par excellence*. It is dominated by the magnificent Norman abbey (see chapter 4) and many people come here to visit Broadlands, the home of the Earl Mountbatten of Burma (see chapter 6).

The main street and the Market Square, with its statue of Lord Palmerston, have some interest and character, while there is an impressive Town Hall of 1866 and Corn Exchange, now a bank. The oldest building in the town is the thirteenth-century house known as King John's Hunting Lodge. It is open to the public as a heritage centre and here one can obtain a town trail which is a useful guide to the exploration of Romsey.

SELBORNE

Selborne is famous as the home of the naturalist Gilbert White. There is the Gilbert White Museum (see chapter 8) and the recreation of the garden so well known through his writings (see chapter 6).

The village of Selborne, with its Norman church, is charmingly picturesque. There are extensive walks up the beech-covered slopes of the 'hanger' with its magnificent views of the village below. At the top is the open space of

Selborne Common, now preserved and maintained by the National Trust. For anyone interested in natural history and the countryside, Selborne is a must on any itinerary in Hampshire.

SOUTHAMPTON

Southampton is not widely perceived as an historic town but it possesses some of the finest old buildings in Britain. For those on the trail of England's heritage, a day spent in Southampton is a most rewarding experience (see also chapters 3, 4, 5, 6 and 8). The town now serves as a regional commercial and shopping centre and is well placed as a base from which to explore the rest of Hampshire.

The archaeology of the Roman town and the now famous Saxon town of Hamwic is displayed in the Museum of Archaeology (see chapter 8). Southampton grew rich on trade with France during the middle ages and there are extensive remains of the merchants' houses, the medieval commercial buildings (see chapter 6) and the unique town defences, built in the fourteenth century with the introduction of artillery in mind (see chapter 5).

The old town contains many fascinating buildings in picturesque settings. Although badly bombed, the High Street still has some gems such as the Dolphin Hotel, while the old town around St Michael's Square and Bugle Street is well worth a visit. Here there is St Michael's church (see chapter 4) and the Tudor House Museum and Garden (see chapter 6).

One of the aspects of the modern town is the opening up of the historic waterfront. There is a marina proposed for the old Town Quay area at the bottom of High Street and Ocean Village can be found in the Old Docks. Ocean Village is a leisure and shopping centre on the waterfront, looking out at yachts moored where liners used to leave for all parts of the world. Names such as *Queen Mary* and *Queen Elizabeth* are part of how the world sees Southampton. Something of the rich maritime story is displayed in the Maritime Museum, housed in the medieval Wool House near the Royal Pier (see chapter 8).

To the north of the old town is the shopping centre of Above Bar where rather drab postwar buildings have been improved by the construction of an extensive pedestrian precinct. The availability of so many large stores is a great convenience. In addition, one of the remarkable aspects of Southampton is the extent of the parks which reach all around the shopping centre. These were the common fields of the medieval town, preserved as parks in the Victorian era, despite the pressure on land from the expansion of the town. About a mile (1½ km) to the north of Above Bar is the Common, 368 acres (149 ha) of open land in the heart of a busy modern city.

STEVENTON

The visitor coming into Hampshire along the great artery of the M3 will pass close to .Steventon, near Basingstoke. It is a place of pilgrimage, for Steventon was Jane Austen's birthplace.

The church is largely thirteenth-century but there is a Saxon cross shaft with carving that dates it to the late ninth century.

STOCKBRIDGE

If the Test valley had a capital then it would be Stockbridge, mecca of anglers for many generations. It has a wide and impressive main street, with the Grosvenor Hotel at its centre. At the east end of the street there is the chancel of the thirteenth-century church, which was replaced in the 1860s by the new church of St Peter.

Stockbridge acquired notoriety in the nineteenth century as the home of the Stockbridge Races which took place on the downs to the west, where the old grandstand survives in splendid isolation amongst acres of ploughed fields.

Nearby is the iron age hillfort of Danebury (see chapter 3).

TITCHFIELD

Titchfield must have been important in the Saxon period as it had a large minster, the tower of which survives in the porch of the present church (chapter 4). Its significance in the middle ages was based on its position at the entrance to the Meon valley and the proximity of Titchfield Abbey (see chapter 4). As well as being a market town, Titchfield was a small port, although in the seventeenth century a wall was built across the mouth of the river and large areas of the sea marsh behind were reclaimed. This means that Titchfield is now inland.

Much of the medieval street pattern of the village, which almost became a small town, survives today. Many of the streets are narrow but the High Street is wide and quite impressive. The predominant style is Georgian red brick which gives as pleasing an effect as in Fareham High Street.

WARNFORD

One of the charming villages of the Meon valley, Warnford had a large house which was demolished some years ago. Two features survive in the park which are worth visiting. The first is the church (see chapter 4) and the second is the remains of the thirteenth-century King John's House (see chapter 6).

WHITCHURCH

Now that it has a bypass, Whitchurch can be appreciated as a small market town where five roads meet. One of the Saxon treasures of Hampshire is to be found in the local church (see chapter 4).

The medieval settlement grew up around a bridge over the river Test and it has been the river that has provided much of the wealth of the town. In the late seventeenth century Henri Portal came here to start paper mills for the production of bank notes, an industry that remains to the present day. The river also powers the silk mill, which was built in the early nineteenth century and still provides silk for, amongst others, the legal profession. The mill is now open to the public (see chapter 7).

WICKHAM

Whether this is a large village or a small town is a matter for debate. Certainly it is one of the most attractive places in rural Hampshire, with its wide open square, flanked by seventeenth- and eighteenth-century brick houses. On each side of the square, houses and shops group to form an almost perfect townscape.

Wickham was probably one of the planned towns developed by the Bishops of Winchester in the thirteenth century, and its square was almost certainly laid out to provide a space for the market and fair granted in 1268. The town was the birthplace of the great medieval churchman and statesman, William of Wykeham, who became Chancellor of England and Bishop of Winchester, and who founded Winchester College and New College, Oxford. Bridge Street curves away eastwards from the square towards the bridge over the river Meon. Here there is the Chesapeake Mill of 1820 which contains timbers taken from the American man o' war, *Chesapeake*, captured by the British in 1813.

WINCHESTER

Winchester is historically, geographically, administratively and spiritually the heart of Hampshire. Any visit to Winchester must take the best part of a day as there is so much to see (see also chapter 3, 4, 5, 6 and 8). An itinerary for Winchester can be constructed in three parts: Winchester as a town, its architecture and archaeology; Winchester and its military heritage; and Winchester and its ecclesiastical history.

The study of Winchester as a town must start with a walk up the High Street, which follows the line of the main east-west street of the Roman town, of the Saxon town founded by Alfred the Great, and then of the medieval town, which was for a time the royal and ecclesiastical capital of England. The Broadway is dominated by the statue of Alfred by Hamo Thornycroft, erected in 1901. The High Street gradually narrows until it becomes a pedestrian precinct at the covered way called the Pentice. There are buildings of many periods in the High Street, but the latest ones seem to blend in with the older ones to maintain the unique quality of this thoroughfare.

Streets run north and south from the High Street following lines established when the town was refounded as a regional capital under Alfred the Great. Near the Buttercross one can pass through a passage to The Square, where the City Museum displays the history and archaeology of Winchester from its Roman origins to the present day (see chapter 8).

At the top of the High Street is the Westgate, one of two surviving medieval gates into the walled city. This is a good place to start a tour of Winchester's military heritage. Soon after the Norman conquest a castle was built in the south-west corner of the town (see chapter 5) and the Castle Hall, with its Round Table, is but a short walk from the Westgate. This part of Winchester was taken over by Charles II, who intended to build a palace to rival Versailles. The main building, designed by Wren, was finished but was taken over for use by the military soon after the death of the King. The use of the site as a barracks has continued until very recent times. There are several military museums of note in this part of Winchester (see chapter 8).

The south-east quarter of the walled town has been principally an ecclesiastical enclosure since the ninth century. The present cathedral is on the site of the Saxon Old Minster which was demolished when the Norman church was built (see chapter 4). From the City Museum one walks through a newly planted avenue of limes to the west front of the cathedral. One can either explore the cathedral or pass through a passageway into The Close, a picturesque grouping of post-Reformation houses on the site of the original claustral buildings (see chapter 4). Near an impressive timber-framed building called Cheyne Court there is a gate leading out of The Close near the medieval Kingsgate. Through Kingsgate one passes out of the walled town into Kingsgate Street with its picturesque grouping of medieval and eighteenth-century houses. This is probably the prettiest part of Winchester. Much of this area is occupied by Winchester College, which was founded in 1382 and is still a leading public school. Conducted tours around the buildings, including the fifteenth-century chantry and cloisters, are available.

From the College there is a charming walk past Wolvesey Castle (see chapter 5) to the river Itchen and, thence, through a park called The Weirs, to the start of the tour at King Alfred's statue.

HAMPSHIRE

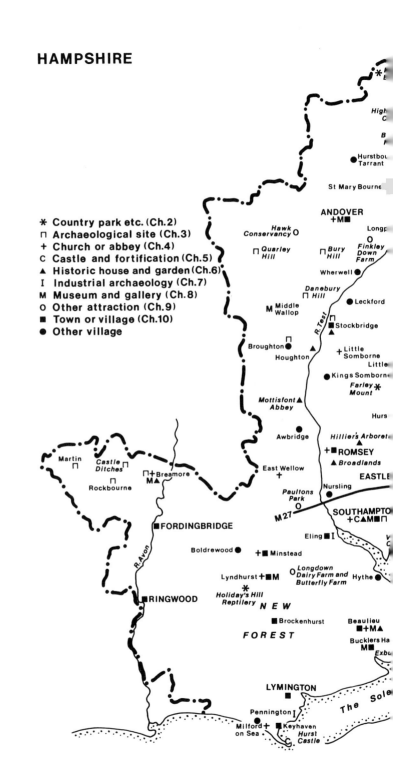

* Country park etc. (Ch.2)
⊓ Archaeological site (Ch.3)
+ Church or abbey (Ch.4)
C Castle and fortification (Ch.5)
▲ Historic house and garden (Ch.6)
I Industrial archaeology (Ch.7)
M Museum and gallery (Ch.8)
O Other attraction (Ch.9)
■ Town or village (Ch.10)
● Other village

*
E

High
C

B
I

● Hurstbou
Tarrant

St Mary Bourne

ANDOVER
+M■

Longp

Hawk O
Conservancy

O
Finkley
Down
Farm

⊓ Quarley
Hill

⊓ Bury
Hill

Wherwell

Danebury
⊓ Hill

● Leckford

M Middle
Wallop

Stockbridge
▲

R.Test

Broughton ●
Houghton

⊓

▲

+ Little
Somborne
Little

● Kings Somborne

Farley *
Mount

Mottisfont ▲
Abbey

Hurs

Awbridge ●

Hilliers Arboret
▲

Martin
⊓

Castle ⊓
Ditches

⊓

Rockbourne

⊓+Breamore
M▲

+■ROMSEY
▲ Broadlands

East Wellow
+

EASTLE

Nursling

Paultons
Park
O

M27

SOUTHAMPTO
+C▲M■■⊓

■FORDINGBRIDGE

Eling ■I

R.Avon

Boldrewood ●

+■ Minstead

Longdown
O Dairy Farm and Hythe
Butterfly Farm

Lyndhurst +■M

*
Holiday's Hill
Reptilery N E W

■RINGWOOD

■ Brockenhurst

Beaulieu
■+M▲

F O R E S T

Bucklers Ha
M■
Exbu

LYMINGTON
■

Pennington I

The Sol e

Milford +
on Sea

■Keyhaven
Hurst
Castle

Index

Page numbers in italic refer to illustrations